T0065157

LIVING IN GOD'S LAUGHTER

DORIS M. SCHOENHOFF

ARCHWAY
PUBLISHING

Archway Publishing books may be ordered through booksellers or by contacting:

Archway Publishing
1663 Liberty Drive
Bloomington, IN 47403
www.archwaypublishing.com
844-669-3957

Cover Image Credit: Fr. Mark Dolan
Interior Image Credit: Doris M. Schoenhoff

ISBN: 978-1-6657-3772-2 (sc)
ISBN: 978-1-6657-3773-9 (e)

Library of Congress Control Number: 2023901647

Print information available on the last page.

Archway Publishing rev. date: 03/28/2023

DEDICATION

In memory of my mother, Anna Duff Schoenhoff, who alone raised three children in a small one-bedroom home, yet still provided what was most necessary: nourishment, education, faith, and love.

DORIS WITH ROLAND AND MARY ANN (TWINS)

The child laughing in the buggy became a woman
who saw laughter as essential to life and faith.

CONTENTS

PREFACE

The COVID-19 pandemic changed and challenged our daily lives. Nothing is quite the same. Still, it has given some of us more time to reflect on life, tap into old experiences, and remember laughter in other difficult times. My life began under unpromising circumstances, but even as a child, I wanted to see as much of the world as possible. That aspiration came true. In 2021, I took the time to write some short memoirs—what I called Travel Tales—for members of my family. Some of those stories are included here, not in the order of time but in the elusive order of heart and mind. They reveal something about me but mostly about people from other countries and other cultures. Many of them touched my life, and some became friends.

In 1993, my book, *The Barefoot Expert*, was published. It was about knowledge systems, those programmed for computers and those in the minds and cultures of indigenous people. A few years later, I was asked by UNESCO to submit an article, which I did—*Catching Dreams on the Web*. As a result, I received an email from Bunker Roy, a remarkable man who started *Barefoot College* in India. Through *Barefoot College*, women in the poorest villages, most of whom could not read or write, learned how to install solar panels and water pumps, changes that would improve their lives and those of their neighbors. Bunker invited me to India, but said, with his sense of humor, that I could not help with the work because I was "too educated." Of course, I understood. At times, education can get in the way of necessity and imagination! While I never made it to India, I continue to admire Bunker's efforts and respect for the poor.

Surprisingly, in 1995, I received a Fulbright Award[1] to pursue my interest in computer technology in a culture different from my own. My tenure, however, did not begin until early 1996. It was an exciting time to be in South Africa while Nelson Mandela was president.[2] A journal, again created at that time for my family, is offered here with minor edits. From informality, often a better truth arises.

As for me, I have navigated my life with laughter. Harmless laughter is grace. God is in us, and we are in God. So, laughter must be in God too. Certainly, it would be difficult to imagine Jesus not laughing, especially at wedding feasts or invited dinners, and not evoking laughter at times with his parables and sermons. Was there laughter when Jesus said the meek were blessed and would inherit the earth? There likely would be today.

Sometimes, laughter might even save lives. The 1997 movie *Life is Beautiful* was partially based on the autobiography of an Italian Jew, Rubino Salmonì, deported to Auschwitz in occupied Poland during World War II. Roberto Benigni's character, Guido, tries to shelter his young son, Giosuè, from the pain and horror of a similar camp in northern Italy. He does this by moving outside his grief to create a game mimicking life in the camp and reviving laughter in his son. At this moment, my thoughts are with the children of Ukraine, that

---

[1] The Fulbright Program was founded in 1946 by Senator J. William Fulbright. The following quote is from the Forward of *The Fulbright Program: A History*: ". . . the Fulbright Program's mission is to bring a little more knowledge, a little more reason, and a little more compassion into world affairs, and thereby increase the chance that nations will learn at last to live in peace and friendship."

[2] On 10 December 1993, Nelson Mandela received the Nobel Peace Prize in Oslo, Norway. He shared it with Frederik Willem de Klerk, the President of South Africa. Quoting Martin Luther King Jr. in the closing words of his acceptance speech, Mandela said that "humanity can no longer be 'tragically bound to the starless midnight of racism and war.'" Exactly four months later on 10 May 1994, Mandela was inaugurated as the first black President of South Africa. He only served one term, leaving office on 14 June 1999.

someday their laughter, scarcely heard now, will heal the wounds of war for their families, their countrymen, and all who watched from afar as evil spread.

The random memories that follow celebrate the healing of laughter in one uncharted life.

1

MOVING TO NEW ZEALAND

Some unforgettable adventures begin rather conventionally, even in the most conservative of places. In 1977, Touché Ross & Co., a prominent accounting firm, placed an advertisement in *Computerworld*, the leading trade publication in information technology. The ad was soliciting résumés for a hospital project in New Zealand. At the time, I was working as a senior systems analyst and programmer at University Hospital in Jacksonville, Florida. New Zealand had never been a country I had my heart set on visiting. I knew very little about New Zealand except that it was way down in the Southern Hemisphere. Only the tips of Chile and Argentina are closer to Antarctica. Maybe that is what intrigued me. In any event, I sent a résumé. The response was quick, and I flew to Detroit, Michigan for an interview.

The project was to design and program a computer system that would tie all the public hospitals in New Zealand together. It necessarily involved a lot of travel throughout the country's islands—North, South, and Stewart Islands. Not only was the firm recruiting prospects in the US but internationally as well. As it turned out, I was offered a job. This move would be over 8000 miles away, on my own, with no relatives, friends, car, apartment, TV, or map awaiting me at the other end. Instinctively, I realized that nothing the interviewers could say would help me grasp what that move to New Zealand would be like. So, I simply decided to accept the offer and embark on both an adventure and a challenge. I took the proverbial leap of faith!

The usual thing to do at that point would be to start packing my bags and booking a flight. However, with the OK of the project managers in Detroit and Auckland, I opted to go by container ship, never having done that before or even knowing exactly what a container ship was. They are huge cargo ships with large containers filled with just about anything that needs to go from one continent to another, all neatly stacked one upon the other and occupying most of the surface of the ship. Often there are a few cabins for passengers who do not mind a no-frills journey.

On June 8, a Wednesday, I flew to Philadelphia, Pennsylvania. Friends who lived nearby in Laurel Springs, New Jersey picked me up at the airport. For part of the time that I lived in Jacksonville, I rented a room in the home of Grace Smith. With Grace were her daughter, Kippy, and her son-in-law, Danny, who worked for the FBI. Grace was visiting them and seeing me off. The next day, on my own, I went into New York City to get an Australian visa. When that was accomplished, I attended noon Mass at St. Patrick's Cathedral and ate a brown-bagged lunch in Rockefeller Plaza. No, I do not have what neurobiologists call super autobiographical memory. Fortunately, I came across faded letters that recorded those details. There was a time when history depended on letter writing and so did curious human beings. The world learned of Jesus because of letters, like the epistles of Paul, and about the eruption of Vesuvius because of the letters of Pliny the Younger. Later, historians, scientists, and an array of academic disciplines and technologies came along that have enhanced human knowledge over time. Today, of course, there is more information than any human being could assimilate or would want to.

In any event, on the following Friday, my three friends drove me to the Port Newark Container Terminal in New Jersey to board the

S.S. Austral Ensign, owned by the Ferrell Lines. The ship was 813 ft. long, could carry up to 29,500 tons, and cruised at 22.6 knots or about 26 mph. The passenger accommodations were a pleasant surprise. The cabin deck was completely air-conditioned. My cabin could easily have lodged two persons. Maybe that is why there were two large windows, perfect for individual viewing of anything out on the water or up in the skies. It was fortunate that I had all this space because I came on board with seven boxes, three pieces of luggage, and one fishing rod. How does a temporary expatriate know how to pack for the duration? In my case, not very well!

All told, there were ten passengers on board, nine Americans and one Australian, Bob Hayes from Brisbane. Nine of the passengers were retired. That is the reason I was dubbed the baby of the group. In some ways, perhaps, I was, although I saw myself as single, young, and headed for a new job, a new life. Unlike cruise ships, there was no doctor on board the *Austral Ensign.* At the time, I never gave that a thought since my doctor visits were few and far between. I was not even born in a hospital. According to my mother, I entered the world on the living room couch, a ten-month baby who needed the assistance of Dr. Sterling to make my entrance.

There were sunny skies when the *Austral Ensign* departed Port Newark on Saturday at about 10:30 a.m. The ride went smoothly until later that night. As we passed Cape Hatteras National Seashore off the coast of North Carolina, the container ship began to rock. Eventually, the sea calmed down and we skirted by Cuba. By Wednesday, the *Austral Ensign* was approaching the Panama Canal Zone. The first highlight of the trip would be going through the Panama Canal. As it turned out, I experienced more excitement than expected.

Depending on the backlog, it might take a ship eight or more hours to pass through the Panama Canal. Our ship anchored outside the canal because there were ships ahead of us. We were not cleared to start through the canal until the next day. During that wait, passengers could disembark. Some of us decided to use the opportunity for a few hours of sightseeing in San Cristobal.

At about 1:30 in the afternoon, there were eight passengers on the metal gangplank waiting to leave the ship. A rope was securing the stairs, but I could feel a slight sway. By chance, I was midway on the stairs. With both hands on the railings, I was humming a happy tune and dangling my left leg over the step. When the passenger near the bottom of the gangplank stepped onto the landing platform, the rope broke and the gangplank dropped about two feet. None of the seniors were hurt, but I jammed my knee. The pain was so intense that I could not even speak. When the passengers directly behind me could not move forward, they realized something was wrong and shouted for help. A launch pulled up to the side of the ship. Quickly, I was helped on board and taken to a hospital in San Cristobal—not exactly how I had planned my sightseeing.

The doctor in San Cristobal cleared me to resume the voyage but emphasized that I needed to see a doctor again as soon as I arrived in New Zealand. From the hospital, I was transported to a launch. By then, there was rain, and I was unable to step down into the covered portion of the launch. The only option was to park my tail end near the bow and enjoy a midday shower. That afternoon and evening I was in considerable pain and my leg was very swollen. The next day, I was sent back to the hospital in San Cristobal. This time I had to see a surgeon. After x-rays, I was told that my knee would eventually require surgery. The doctor gave me Codeine along with instructions to stay off my feet for ten days and use a cane when I walked.

Fortunately, I arrived on the ship in time to spend from 3:30 p.m. to 10:30 p.m. observing our passage through the Panama Canal. It was fascinating to learn that water and gravity do all the work of lifting and lowering these huge ships through the locks. Water intake and water draining are what it is all about. There were six locks, three up and three down. Surrounding the locks were beautiful lakes and densely vegetated islands. By the time we passed through the last lock, my knee was killing me, but I had to see it all. The next day, I remained in my cabin elevating my badly swollen leg. Meals were brought to me. The captain, who called himself "an old southern boy from Virginia," popped in for visits and rechristened me, Gimpy. For the rest of the trip, I limped about the ship. As for the prediction that I would require knee surgery, that has never come true in the succeeding decades.

We had a party celebrating the crossing of the equator on June 28. The ladies came in cocktail dresses and gowns. All I had in my suitcase were jeans and t-shirts. Not wanting to miss the party, I put on my best jeans and a red t-shirt that I had bought at the Grand Canyon three months prior. On the back of the shirt were big black letters that read "Go Ride a Mule." When the captain saw me, he asked one of the passengers to take my picture, and there was laughter all around, including from me. I said, "Here I wear my best shirt to your party and everyone makes fun!" There is grace in laughing, particularly at oneself, as well as an inner freedom.

Once in open water with no land or lights in sight, I again spent hours every day on the deck, slowly walking its full length. In the day, there were dolphins, flying fish, and birds to spot, like petrels, gulls, and osprey. In the night, there was a vault thick with brilliant stars. Growing up in St. Louis, I never knew the sky could be blanketed with stars. Now I was even able to see the Southern Cross, four major stars arranged in the pattern of a cross with a smaller star in the interior. There are 88 confirmed constellations in our galaxy, and the Southern Cross is the smallest. What I was actually seeing in all the stars was light traveling from far away and long ago. I remember thinking that if I had a giant telescope, I could see thousands of galaxies like fluorescent islands in the darkness of space.

Alone, I had the stars and the sea to myself—a front-row seat as the ship cut through the ocean's surface, leaving its dark mystery deep below. One evening, I was on the deck of the bow, when a watchman and I spotted whale spouts. They were difficult to pick out amidst the water's white caps, but I saw spent breath rising from blowholes. What a thrill to know those intelligent, awesome creatures were nearby! Every day, the captain would ask me, "Have you seen any whales today, Gimpy?" So, that night I left a note in his office.

"To whom do I report my whale sightings? A crewman and I spotted whale spouts off the port side at 1900 hours!" At the cocktail party that Sunday, the captain put his hand on my head, tousled my hair, and said, "I'm sure glad you've got a sense of humor." How often have I heard that in my life!

In the evening, the other passengers preferred cards or conversation in the lounge. Of course, there likely were some "ancient mariners" among them who knew the sea much better than I. Still, I was enamored by it. My thoughts were never about potential danger. That was the stuff of novels and movies. As a Midwesterner and later a Florida transplant, what I knew about life on the water came from observing barges and boats on the Mississippi and Missouri Rivers, as well as surfers and cruise ships along the Florida beaches. Spotting whales and all the varied life that depended on the ocean's bounty added a new dimension to my love of nature.

At meals, we all gathered in a small dining area. One evening, the weather was particularly rough and I was the only one at the table with the captain. Fortunately, at the start of the trip, I had taken what, at that time, astronauts took for motion sickness—or that is what my doctor claimed. The back of the captain's chair was near the wall, but mine faced the open room. As the ship rolled, my chair would roll across the room and then roll back to the table—again and again. We laughed and laughed. I was surprised that such a large ship could wobble. Later I learned that container ships do not have stabilizers like cruise ships, so you feel the rock and roll of the ocean.

During the trip, I also celebrated a birthday. The steward made a special cake, decorated with red roses and my name. When the candles were lit, everyone began singing. That evening, the captain came to the lounge where some of us were talking. "Since I couldn't show you any whales on this trip," he said, "I want you to have this." From behind his back, he produced a beautiful whale's tooth from his collection. It even had a blue bow on it. That whale's tooth still rests on a bookcase in my living room.

As the ship sailed further south, we were able to see some of the

South Pacific Islands in the distance. When we passed through the Society Islands, Huahine was close enough for me to distinguish houses and coconut palms with my binoculars. All around Raiatea was a coral reef. The ocean waves hit the reef instead of the shore. Between the reef and the island was a beautiful emerald lagoon. From a greater distance, I spotted Bora Bora. James Michener served there during World War II, and his book about that experience inspired the musical *South Pacific*. I kept my eyes fixed on Bora Bora until it faded on the horizon. The next morning, I sighted Rarotonga, the largest of the Cook Islands. When I finally came down from the deck, I passed by the captain. At the time, I was wearing jeans, a t-shirt, and a windbreaker. On my head was an old army mechanic's cap that had belonged to a friend of mine who served in India during World War II. He had asked me to take it along on my journeys because I would see what he never had a chance to see. "What a lovely sight," the captain said. "You're going to shake up those New Zealanders!" That brought instant laughter and I was sure my friend would have laughed along with me!

Of course, certain times call for seriousness. On one occasion, the captain called me to his station and said that the ship's navigation system was not working. The system consisted of a Wang calculator. The ship, the captain said in confidence, was out of all communication. How do you reply to that when you are just a passenger and not an intrepid mariner or even a former Girl Scout? Since the captain knew I worked with computers, he asked me to take a look at the navigation manual. I puzzled through the beat-up pages and the strange jargon, but that was not much help. Having given the captain what clues I could, he and his first officer tried again. Who knows where we might have ended up had I put my hand to the Wang? No thanks to my efforts, we did make it safely to Australia—probably by the stars!

The *Austral Ensign* finally pulled into Brisbane on July 1 at 10 a.m. At 4:30 a.m., I was already awake and watching the whole operation, including taking the pilot on board. A local pilot assists the crew with docking. That process can take hours because of the size of a container ship. Tug boats usually coax the ship into place, sometimes pushing it and other times pulling it. Many of us find it challenging to steer a car into a tight parking place much less a ship into a dock.

Docking in Brisbane proved to be the end of the line for me. There was a longshoreman strike in Australia, so our ship was stuck in port. Sometimes, I was told, a strike could go on for weeks. It was time for me to head to New Zealand and get to work. Because I would be flying, I left all my belongings in my cabin except for one suitcase of clothes. When the *Austral Ensign* finally docked in Auckland, I planned to pick up the rest of my luggage.

Shortly before I left the ship, one of the male passengers sitting in the lounge called me over. Unexpectedly, he said that he had a present for me. Then he put quite a few bills on the table—how much it amounted to I do not know. At that point, his wife headed our way and he looked nervous. To save him embarrassment, I took the cap off my head and put it on top of the money. After his wife said good-by, I retrieved my cap, thanked the man for his kind thoughts, and told him that I would be fine. Then, with a smile, I suggested he hang onto that money and have a good time in Australia with his wife.

After leaving the ship, I spent two days visiting my cousins, the MacNamara clan, in Brisbane. Then, I flew to Melbourne to stay with more Irish cousins, the Duff clan. Phil Duff picked me up from the Melbourne Airport in a Jaguar—the first and last time I ever rode in one. Phil was a retired aeronautical engineer who came to Australia after the Second World War on a two-year rocket project and decided to stay. Too soon, it was time for me to fly to New Zealand.

Three weeks later, I inquired why the rest of my luggage had still not arrived in Auckland. An agent at the Auckland Harbor Board said the *Austral Ensign* had problems after leaving Melbourne. The Harbor Board had lost all radio contact with the ship. Around that time, New Zealand had experienced a gale with 80 mph winds off its western coast. The Tasman Sea lies between Australia and New Zealand. The best time to travel on the Tasman Sea is from February to March, definitely not from June to August. That is wintertime down under, a common colloquialism for Australia and New Zealand. The agent told me that, if they could not make contact with the *Austral Ensign* soon, they were going to send out the Coast Guard.

The ship finally did arrive. As I boarded the ship, everyone was happy to see me. I got hugs and kisses from passengers and crew alike. Of course, that was lovely. They invited me to stay for dinner. One of the passengers told me that the captain had not been down for meals the whole week. That is when I heard their firsthand story of the passage to New Zealand. The ship had indeed run into rough weather in the Tasman Sea. At one point, the speed of the *Austral Ensign* was only four knots. Along the way, the radio operator began drinking. Bottles of liquor from the passenger lounge and cabins went missing. Eventually, he reached a point where he was incapacitated. No one else on board could operate the wireless. On top of that predicament, a crewmember died when the ship was midway between Australia and New Zealand. He started hemorrhaging and there was no way to stop the bleeding. After his death, the only alternative was to put his body in the food freezer. That gave new meaning to the line from *The Godfather* about sleeping with the fishes![3]

When all the grizzly details of their ordeal had been relayed, one of the passengers said that it was lucky that I disembarked the ship in Brisbane and missed the rough seas. By that time, the captain was joining us and heard the remark. "Are you kidding?" the captain said. "This nut would've been out there with her binoculars and camera the whole time!" I was glad to see the captain again because we laughed and joked the entire time. Perhaps that helped to ease the tensions he and the passengers had been under. In my case, I do not doubt that friendly laughter lifts the mind and soul.

---

[3] "Luca Brasi sleeps with the fishes." *The Godfather.* Directed by Francis Ford Coppola (1972, Paramount Pictures)

2

THE GOOD SHEPHERD

It was a random meeting—two strangers seated side by side on an Air New Zealand flight. As soon as I spoke, the older gentleman next to me heard my American accent, and that was all it took to spark a conversation. He liked the Yanks, a name I only associated with old movies about World War II. What I learned about New Zealanders is that they entered the war in 1939, right after Germany invaded Poland. They served in the Royal Air Force of Great Britain and fought in southern Europe and northern Africa. The Yanks came on board in 1942.

Of course, the gentleman assumed I was on vacation and wanted to know how I was enjoying his country. Briefly, I explained that I had moved to New Zealand and was working in Auckland. Just for conversation, I shared with him my first experience going to the office. It was a Sunday and I had taken two buses to reach the building where I would report the next day. As I was walking down a slope toward the entrance, a German shepherd came barking and running toward me. Then his mouth clamped down on the left cuff of my coat and pulled me along to a Māori guard hidden from sight behind an entrance panel. After identifying who I was, the guard explained that the dog was trained to protect him and the building during off-hours.

Good dog! As I came to know New Zealanders, I appreciated their balanced sense of work, family, and enjoyment. No one would think of coming to the office on a Sunday. In my case, the German shepherd needed to reinforce that!

My seatmate picked up the conversation and told me that he owned a sheep farm. His wife had died and his children were grown. They had homes nearby but he lived alone. Quite unexpectedly, he invited me to visit his farm and wrote down all his contact information. His name escapes me now, so I will just call him Ben. While our flight was coming to an end, I told Ben that perhaps I might visit him and thanked him for the invitation.

Eventually, I did rent a car, acquire a map, and drive to see Ben. When, according to the map, I was right in his vicinity, I was awed by the bright green earth and gorgeous, snow-covered mountain that seemed to have been dropped all alone from heaven. In the Māori language, it was called Taranaki, meaning "shining mountain." Later I learned that it was a fairly recent volcano. In geological time, it was less than 150,000 years old—practically a youngster. Plus, my first impression of it was not so far-fetched. The Māori tell a story that Taranaki once resided among other volcanic mountains. One day a fight erupted between two of the mountains, Taranaki and Tongariro, over a female mountain, Pihanga. As a result, Taranaki was chased away to live as a lonely bachelor.

If I was amazed by the beauty and presence of Taranaki, I was also surprised by the size of Ben's farm. To the eye, the land seemed to go on forever. His home was inviting and comfortable. Before heading to my room that evening, I was told that in the morning we would go for a ride. Ben provided no other details. After a very early breakfast, we went outside and I saw my transportation. It looked like a small tractor. At the rear was a space where I could stand up, lean over, and hold on to a bar or the back of the driver's seat. This seemed reasonable until we sped off on our sheep chase. Then there were lots of bumps, bounces, and holy smokes!

At one point we spotted a lamb, lying on the grass by itself. Ben stopped the vehicle, dismounted, picked up the lamb, and told me that we had to head back to the house. With Ben snuggling the lamb between his lap and his chest, we drove back. As soon as we went in the back door of his home, Ben began building a fire in a large kitchen fireplace. I remember telling him that I had only seen fireplaces in living rooms but never in a kitchen.

Then Ben took a blanket and spread it on the fireplace tiles. Gently, he placed the lamb on the blanket. As someone who grew up in a city, I asked him, "Why are you doing that when you'll send this lamb to slaughter as it gets older?" His reply was instant. "Because I'm a shepherd and this is my sheep," he said. "What must come later will come, but for now I'll care for my sheep." For a while I was silent, but then I spoke. "It's the gospel come to life," I told Ben. "Like Jesus, you're the good shepherd." In all these years, I have never forgotten that moment. To me, it was more powerful than any Sunday sermon I have ever heard on the Good Shepherd from city priests who, understandably, have only known lamb on a menu.

When the weekend was over and I was leaving to drive back to Auckland, Ben's daughter stopped by. She seemed a little surprised to see me but pleased. Of course, I was excited to tell her about hitching a ride on the tractor and the successful rescue of the lamb. That was the only time I visited Ben and his sheep. Yet, the memory remains indelible.

Historically, sheep were brought to New Zealand by Captain Cook, the British explorer, in 1773. At the time I lived in New Zealand, 1978-1981, there were about 3.2 million people while the sheep population was at its all-time high of 70.3 million sheep. According to a United Nations estimate posted on 1 July 2022, the population of New Zealand has risen to about five million. The sheep population, on the other hand, has declined to approximately 26.7 million. All things considered, I experienced a true baa-baa-blessing of sheep!

As New Zealand turned out to be my jumping-off point for other travel adventures, it was serendipity that I briefly met David

Attenborough there. This was a few years before he became Sir David through his many BBC nature documentaries. Known for his adventurous life, he continues to speak out about climate change and other threats to Earth even in his mid-nineties.

My introduction to Attenborough was at a book signing. Before he autographed his book *Life on Earth*, he asked me, "Did you know there is a sea slug named Doris?" No, I did not. Perhaps if I knew more about sea slugs, I could be thrilled with that knowledge. Attenborough said my namesake is *Doris odhneri*. Then, as he signed my copy of the book, he suggested, "You really should take a look at it."

I did just that. *Doris odhneri* is found from Kenai Peninsula, Alaska, to Point Loma, California. One of its common names is "giant white dorid." Now that is getting personal! Attenborough was right, of course. Doris is stunningly white, beautifully compact, and very charming.

No doubt that, like my marine counterpart, I am a sea slug compared to David Attenborough and his many travels around the world and up-close to wildlife. Yet, what I have experienced of the earth's beauty, both in nature and with fellow humans, has been all grace and much laughter.

3

AIR NEW ZEALAND
FLIGHT 901

New Zealand is one of the most beautiful countries in the world. Rolling green hills, pristine lakes, mountains, glaciers, active volcanoes . . . all as close to heaven on earth as you can get. Moviegoers know it from Peter Jackson's *Lord of the Rings* trilogy (2001-2003). Of my time there, I have many wonderful memories, but one that is dark, and incomprehensible, yet immersed in faith.

In 1979 Air New Zealand was offering four sightseeing flights over Antarctica. The airline had begun these limited flights in 1977. Chile is the closest country to Antarctica but New Zealand is a good jumping-off place as well. The flights would take off from Auckland on four successive Wednesdays in November—dates 7, 14, 21, and 28.

Initially, I booked the flight for November 21, but then I learned that Edmund Hillary would narrate the expedition on November 28. In 1953, Hillary, a New Zealander, and his Sherpa guide, Tenzing Norgay, were the first confirmed individuals to reach the summit of Mount Everest. For over twenty years, Hillary had been a hero not only in New Zealand but internationally. I was considering rescheduling my flight. Of course, another option would be to take both flights.

On November 21, I boarded my scheduled flight. To reach Antarctica would take about eight hours. The flight was, as expected, exhilarating. The pilot flew low over McMurdo Sound and I snapped good photos of mountains, glaciers, and other features of the Antarctic landscape. I was also surprised how the pilot would dip a wing to give us better visibility. When he dipped the wing, everyone standing would slide to one side of the plane. I crashed into a few people several times on those dips and was buffeted as well. The trip was a real adventure.

After returning to Auckland, I decided to take the trip on November 28 as well. Meeting Edmund Hillary and listening to his stories would be a rare opportunity. However, for some reason, I changed my mind and told the booking agent that I would not go on the next trip. During the following week, I had doubts and thought I made a mistake, but I did not call the booking agent.

On 28 November 1979, Air New Zealand Flight 901 took off from Auckland. It never returned. The pilot, in poor visibility conditions, flew the plane into Mount Erebus, the southernmost active volcano on earth. All 257 people on board the plane were killed. Some of the bodies were never recovered. As it turned out, Edmund Hillary was not on the flight. He asked his friend and climbing partner, Peter Mulgrew, to take his place. Hillary had a speaking engagement in the US. About ten years later, Hillary married the widow of Peter Mulgrew. Sometimes shared tragedy binds people together tighter than anything else. Perhaps this was the case.

The news of the tragedy had a chilling effect on New Zealand. It was as though every New Zealander knew someone on that flight. In St. Louis, my brother heard the news on TV but was afraid to tell my mother. She was aware of my plans to take the second Antarctic flight. Of course, I phoned home and both of them were relieved to finally hear my voice.[4]

Almost immediately, there was an inquiry. Anyone who had photos from the previous Antarctic flights was asked to submit them. As I recall, we could also submit a description of the trip. I did both and attended as many of the hearings as I could without interfering with my job. Gradually, more information surfaced from the inquiry and the press. Captain Jim Collins and copilot Greg Cassin had never flown to Antarctica before. Some concluded that pilot error was the cause of the tragedy.

A second investigation determined that was not the case. A Royal Commission of Inquiry conducted by Justice Peter Mahon QC ultimately provided the families of the victims with a different explanation for the plane crash. Mahon's report on 27 April 1981 exonerated the crew. The cause of the crash was attributed to Air New Zealand. Collins and Cassin entered the flight coordinates into the navigation computer the night before takeoff. A ground crew altered the coordinates very early the next morning; they corrected an error that had been overlooked in the previous flights. Collins and Cassin were not notified of the change. In reduced visibility, the captain and copilot thought they were flying over McMurdo Sound but they were flying into Mount Erebus. The crash of ANZ 901 is still the worst peacetime disaster in New Zealand's history.

Recounting this tragedy of Air New Zealand Flight 901 brought back a related memory. On 11 September 2001, I drove to Syracuse Hancock International Airport in New York for an early morning flight. Shortly after 9:00 a.m., my plane was preparing to taxi. After I had settled in my seat on the aisle and clipped my seat belt, the man

---

[4] The plane was a McDonnell Douglas DC10-30 (ZK-NZP). It was built at the McDonnell Douglas plant in Long Beach, California. Corporate headquarters were in St. Louis, Missouri. My brother, Roland, spent his entire career there as an aerospace engineer and, ultimately, a director. As someone who loved the company and took his work seriously, he was relieved to learn that no structural failures in the plane contributed to the horrific accident.

next to me began talking on his phone. "What? What?" Suddenly the pilot announced that everyone had to exit the plane immediately. There was a lot of noise with people talking on phones and pushing into the aisles. When I reached the exit door, I asked the stewardess what was happening. She was panicky. "Planes are falling from the sky," she said. "Get out, get out."

It took several days before any flights were departing again from Syracuse. Fortunately, I spent the time at the home of a longtime friend, Carole Rightnour. At one point, I naively suggested we drive to New York City to volunteer in any way we could. The news made it clear that tunnels and bridges heading into the city were closed to nonessential traffic. As soon as possible, I booked a flight to St. Louis. On take-off, there were no occupied seats in first class; less than a dozen passengers were in coach. A steward came up to me and asked if I wanted to sit in first class. I smiled and said, "I think I have plenty of room right here." Then he asked if I would like one of the aircraft pins that were usually offered to children. I replied, "Sure." He dropped the whole bag of pins in my lap. We laughed like children playing in our own reality. The pins remain on a shelf in my home. Ultimately, the 9/11 death toll was 2750 people in New York City, 184 at the Pentagon, and 40 on a field in Pennsylvania.

One tragedy was the result of human error; the other of human evil. Both were unfathomable; both impacted an entire nation. Since these incidents, I often think about grace—not about luck, happenstance, or probability. Well, it is not so much that I think as that I wonder. Socrates said that wonder is the beginning of wisdom. Sometimes wonder is all that you can do. Sometimes wonder is as far as you can go.

4

ISLAND HOPPING

During my three years in New Zealand, I lived in two privately owned residences. Both were in Kohimarama, a suburb of Auckland on the North Island. From there, the view of Auckland Harbor, now called Waitematā Harbor, was striking. In the distance, one could also see several islands, actually extinct volcanoes. That view and walks along the promenade motivated me to look for an apartment there.

My first apartment was at 70 Kohimarama Road in a large two-story house that had been converted into four dwellings, although for most of my stay only three of us were living there. Mrs. McGregor owned and resided at the residence in an upstairs apartment. Her name always reminded me of Beatrix Potter's tales about Peter Rabbit and his nemesis, Mr. McGregor. Mrs. McGregor was a combination of good humor and fierce politics. Frequently, she voiced her opinion of Prime Minister Robert Muldoon, who was known for his brawling style of governing.

Miss Ferby, whose apartment was also upstairs, was a retired bookkeeper—a pleasant, brisk-walking, no-nonsense woman who enjoyed playing Mahjong. She offered to teach me Mahjong and bring me along to one of the regular matches with her friends. Consisting of

144 tiles with Chinese symbols, the game is not for those with short attention spans. It requires a rigorous skill set that includes tactics, observation, memory, and strategies. At the time, it seemed to me that I got enough of that at the office, so I passed on a chance to be trained in Mahjong by an aficionado or close to it.

In my last year in New Zealand, my apartment was on the unfinished bottom level of a two-story private home at 120 Selwyn Avenue, just a couple of minutes from Mrs. McGregor's front door. The owners of the home, a husband and wife, lived on the upper level. My level had a pleasant bedroom right off the front entrance, while the rest of the level was concrete floors and unfinished walls, punctuated with wooden posts, and decorated with a water heater, a breaker panel, a lawnmower, tools, and such. In the far back right-hand corner was a small bathroom. You could say the décor was home-repair monastic.

When I decided to return to the States, I wanted to see more of the world on my way home. Opportunity knocked! My landlord worked for the New Zealand Customs Service and was able to get me passage on a Royal New Zealand Navy ship headed to Fiji. The RNZN had maritime roles and also supported the Customs Service. A naval officer, scheduled for this particular mission, had taken sick, and his cabin was vacant. Happily, I was offered his cabin (the only woman on board), and my passage was free.

The ship departed on the evening of November 5, Guy Fawkes Day. In 1605, a group of Catholics attempted to blow up the British Houses of Parliament and kill King James I. The Gun Powder Plot, as it was called, was a protest against Protestant rule. Fawkes planted 36 barrels of gunpowder under the palace, but they were discovered. When Fawkes was arrested, he was sentenced to be hanged. Instead, he either stumbled or jumped off the gallows and broke his neck. In England, they celebrate Guy Fawkes Day with fireworks. New Zealand does the same.[5] As our ship pulled out of Auckland Harbor,

---

[5] New Zealand became a Dominion of the British Empire in 1907. After the death of Queen Elizabeth II on 8 September 2022, King Charles III became New Zealand's titular monarch.

there were bursting fireworks up above. It was like a special send-off celebration!

Often on the journey, I would stand on the deck of the ship and scan the ocean for whales or dolphins. There was a steward on the ship who was from the Lau Group, the most remote islands of the Fiji Archipelago. The people there are a mixture of Melanesian and Polynesian cultures. When I stood on the deck watching the waves and the ocean life, this steward would come up and talk to me in simple, broken English about where he was born. He told me that elderly people in his village were cared for and revered. Also, if someone in need came up to you and asked for your shirt and your sandals, you must give them to that person with generosity and not ask for them to be returned. It reminded me of Jesus' words to his disciples and the crowd that gathered around him. "Give to everyone who asks you, and if anyone takes what belongs to you, do not demand it back."[6] This conversation with the steward made me determined to visit the Lau Islands.

After I disembarked the RNZN ship in Viti Levu, the largest island in the Republic of Fiji, I took a taxi to a hotel. On the way, the driver wanted to show me what he said was a beautiful spot. There was a pond in a lush and secluded area. He said that people liked to come there and skinny-dip. Then he asked me if I would like to join him in the pool. My response was clear enough and firm enough that he got back on the main road and headed to the hotel.

When I checked into my room, a housekeeper was still finishing up. We spoke briefly and, before departing, she let me know about sex services that could be arranged for guests. I was beginning to wonder what type of impression Americans had made on Fiji. Or, possibly, it was just what I attracted on my low-budget tour of the South Pacific. Anyway, I concentrated on leaving Fiji and going to the Lau Islands.

After checking out of my hotel, I went to the docks to ask how I could get to the Lau Islands. At first, I was told that I could go on a

---

[6] Luke 6:30 NIV

medical ship, but that plan had to be scrapped because of a medical emergency. Continuing my search, I did find a boat that was going to one of the Lau Islands, and I boarded it. Once again, I was the only woman on the boat. Did you ever see *The African Queen*, a classic movie with Humphrey Bogart and Katherine Hepburn?[7] Well, the boat I set foot on was bigger than *The African Queen* but it competed with it for shabbiness. It seemed to function as a barter vessel. The boat would transport items from Viti Levu, and the Lau islanders would barter for them with fruits, livestock, or crafts.

My cabin was very small, had no lock on the door, and no glass in the window through which I stared out at the sea. The crew members, who spoke very little English, would walk the deck, pass by my window, poke their heads in, and say, "Hallo, hallo." At my first meal, the cook put a boiled chicken—head, beak, wattles, comb, toenails, eyes . . . the whole chicken anatomy—on the serving platter. For the rest of the trip, I opted for fruit, crackers, and jelly, even though I did see a roach climbing in and out of the large jelly tin.

Eventually, of course, you have to shower even though I tried to stretch out the aromatic time limit. When I did finally start to open the narrow door to the make-do shower on the boat, I heard grunts, squeals, and snorts, but never quite an oink, oink. As a result, I was surprised to see a large pig tied to the shower arm. I was not sure what to do next except to strip off my clothes, turn on the water, and shower with the pig. Since I suspect that was the first shower that pig ever had, I am sure he was mystified as well!

In the South Pacific, tropical cyclones can occur from November to April. Unfortunately, our boat ended up on the edge of one. That night I will never forget. As I lay on the bunk in my cabin with my hands clutching the sides of the bunk, waves of water came through my open window and drenched me and everything else. The storm went on through the night, with the boat rocking. Of course, I thought

---

[7] *The African Queen*. Directed by John Huston (1951, United Artists). In 1994, *The African Queen* was selected for preservation in the National Film Registry of the Library of Congress.

I was going to die. It was glorious to see the sun the next day and know that everyone on board was safe—including the pig.

We were now within the Lau Group and dropped anchor by one of the islands. It was Sunday and I disembarked for the day. People from the island began coming up to me. One woman held her dark arm next to mine and said "beautiful, beautiful." I touched her arm and said "beautiful, beautiful." Someone else took me by the hand and led me to the hut of their chief. Wearing a t-shirt and cutoff jeans, I was not properly dressed for island royalty.

The chief indicated a wooden chest that he wanted me to sit on. Then he took some fragrant oil and began rubbing it on my arms, legs, and even my hair. I smiled but had no idea what was going on. Gradually, I surmised it was a ritual act of anointing. With hindsight, I concede that I was likely rather smelly after life on the boat—and showers with a pig!

There was no doubt, though, that the chief was dressed for some ceremonial occasion. He led me out of his hut and to another building which was a church with a cross on top. Then I realized that it was Sunday! The chief pointed to a door and said, "People." I turned to go in, but he took my arm, tugged me toward another entrance, and said "Chief." Inside the church, people were seated on wooden benches. The chief and I were seated facing the congregation. I remember there was singing and a sermon. Most of all, I remember a man with a big switch. When any of the children or adults misbehaved, he would snap that switch over their heads and, I suspect, on exposed body parts as well. Fortunately, since I was seated by the chief, I was outside of his jurisdiction! The service was reverent and ceremonial.

Later in the day, I was invited to sit cross-legged in a circle on the ground. The circle consisted of men only. They passed around a wooden bowl that had a liquid resembling something out of the Muddy Mississippi. Even though I did not want to taste it, I raised the bowl to my lips, took a sip, and passed it to the person on my left. In retrospect, I wish I had asked about the significance of the ceremony. Perhaps it was an initiation rite or, maybe, a ceremonial toast. If so, it is the one and only toast I have ever had! When we rose and expressed our goodbyes, I headed back to the boat. Before I left, though, I raised my camera to take a picture of the chief. All of a sudden, other islanders began appearing in my camera lens. Each time I thought I was ready to take the shot, more would come out of hiding and I would step back a few more paces. Eventually, I did snap the photo.

When I arrived on board the boat and evening was softening the light, the men on the boat were heading out again for some festivities on the island—all the men. Some asked me if I wanted to join them, but I declined. Since the crew was disembarking, the skipper told me that he had put a lantern on the side of the boat. The men would watch the lantern from the island to make sure the anchored boat did not float away. Then they climbed into small landing crafts and paddled out to the island. It was a strange feeling to know I was indeed all alone on this moored boat. As the evening stretched later and later, I could still hear faint sounds of song and laughter from the island. Apparently, I alone was ready for sleep, so I stretched out on my bunk. At some point in the darkness, I could hear the men coming back to the boat and singing as they climbed on board. When they approached my window, their voices became a whisper. With no sense of fear or danger, I thought about how considerate they were as they tried not to wake me.

After that adventure, our boat returned to Viti Levu. However, more island adventures by air lay ahead. In Rarotonga, I rented a motorbike. When I told the attendant that I had never ridden one before, he was understandably worried. After a brief instruction in gears and brakes, I mounted the bike. Then I warned him, "Better get out of the way," and took off. To my surprise, I did not tumble over but ended up circling the island twice. Of course, it only takes about an hour to circle it once! Along the way, I had thoughts like, "Why didn't I ride one of these years ago?" escalating to "Maybe I should buy one when I get back home." I did not.

Later I was able to visit Bora Bora, the beautiful island that I had watched from afar on board the *Austral Ensign*. One island is memorable, though, not for its beauty but its mystery—Easter Island (Rapa Nui). Compared to Bora Bora, Easter Island appeared almost barren. When you look across the landscape, you realize that trees are missing, not totally but enough to get your attention. Of course, visitors do not come to Easter Island for landscaping. They come to see the strange figures that dot the landscape. The moai are monolithic figures carved from volcanic rock possibly in 1200-1500 AD. Actually, many unfinished moai remain in the quarry at Rano Raraku, a volcanic crater. The carvers may have noticed a flaw in the rock they were chiseling, or perhaps some of the carvings were not intended to be totally freed from the crater. In any event, it would take a geologist to explain how igneous rock could last as long as the moai.[8]

For whatever reason, there was only a scattering of tourists on Easter Island when I visited. One day when I set out in a rental car, there was no one else around. It was an unexpected gift to have both solitude and mystery spread out before me. When I climbed up one of the hills, I ended up stumbling and tumbling down, finally slamming into one of the moai. Fortunately, no bones were broken and no ankles were sprained. That was an unanticipated experiment to prove the hardness of volcanic rock over time!

One of my memories of Easter Island remains enigmatic. On a subsequent outing, I was with three or four other tourists. A guide, with limited English, was pointing out an unusual rock formation on a hillside. Part of the rock jutted out and was flattened; in its center was a hole. The shape appeared to be partially carved rather than wholly eroded, but that was only my guess. The guide seemed to indicate that this rock formation may have been used to check for virginity in a female. As he directed his attention to me, his words and

---

[8] Once when I was in Christchurch, New Zealand for a meeting, I stopped by the cathedral of the same name. Two stonecutters were chiseling stones for the cathedral restoration. Of course, given my personality, I went up to speak with them. One said that when the stone came from the quarry it was soft. However, after it was exposed to the weather, its molecular structure changed and it became very hard. In the stone cutter's hands, the stone appeared to cut very easily. If offered, I would have picked up a chisel and mallet myself to experiment!

gestures became frustrating while my face remained stoic. Finally, he gave up. Perhaps he thought that I did not understand what he was saying. I did but was at a loss for words or questions. It reminded me of medieval stories about a "pope chair" which supposedly was used to determine if the papal candidate was a female trying to sneak by. Best to remain silent and inscrutable like a moai!

CHIEF AND FAMILY

VILLAGERS GATHERED FOR PHOTO

TWO CHILDREN BY THE CHURCH

MOAI

5

DIPPING INTO EUROPE

My trips, as with my life in general, have usually evoked laughter, sometimes only my own. Generally, they have been to less-traveled countries, particularly for their remote landscapes, wildlife, and culture. However, my few trips to Europe provided a different kind of adventure and, admittedly, some slapstick humor. In one instance, a friend and I had departed from the US on different airlines, at different times, and for different destinations. However, we planned to meet at Luxembourg Airport on the same day and at approximately the same time. What could go wrong?

As it turned out, I arrived as scheduled since Luxembourg was my original destination, but my friend did not. After spending a few days in England, she took a ferry to Bruges, Belgium, to visit an art museum or two. Later, she boarded a train for Luxembourg Airport. That ride took much longer than she expected. Of course, I was unaware of all the adjustments in Plan A and there was no Plan B. Oh, forget about smartphones—they were penciled in for a future century!

After waiting for hours, I left the airport to find a nearby hotel. Then I drove back to the airport and remained until the airline agents began to close down their counters. The puzzle was "how do I leave a note?" Well, I asked the last agent manning one of the counters to lend me paper and a ballpoint pen. Then I resorted to plastering pieces of paper with my name, hotel, and room number on prominent surfaces in the terminal. Amazingly, this no-tech solution worked and produced a knock on the door of my hotel room in the middle of the night—fortunately from my friend and not a scary stranger. This, however, was only the start of more surprises to come.

At a café in a French village, where we stopped for lunch, I was trying to tell a waitress what I wanted to order. To simplify things, I went to the front window where various pastries were displayed, raised my hand to the very top shelf, and pointed to what looked to me like a pizza. Inexplicably, my fingertips swept the pastry up and airborne. Speechless, I watched it slowly slide down the window glass, leaving a smear of sauce and unidentifiable fillings. The waitress spoke little English and I spoke no French. She was angry as she picked up the pastry that had settled comfortably on the window sill with some of it oozing over the side. With precision, she folded the corners of the pastry together like a box, raised one hand, and motioned for me to leave. That instruction was conveyed with such authority that I suspected she was the café owner. As I tried to apologize and offered to pay for the demolished pastry, I also cupped my hand over my mouth to stifle my laughter. Not a good sign of contrition! It all unfolded like a scene from a comedy. As I recall, my friend missed most of the drama. She was sitting at the table looking over the menu, unaware that lunch would not be served, at least not in that café. Soon enough, she got the picture.

There were more misadventures ahead: handing off car keys in a hotel elevator, only to hear them "clink, clink" down the elevator shaft; getting locked in a creepy restroom at a gas station and waiting, waiting for rescue; stumbling into a tall candle stand in a cathedral sanctuary with browsing tourists and catching it in descent, like a dancer with a partner in a deep dip. Overall, my friend and I sped across the tourist sites of Europe for about ten days. When we returned the rental vehicle, the agent checked the mileage and said, "Did you ever get out of the car?" That was the only time that my friend suggested going on a vacation with me. Yes, one could politely call that a coincidence!

In any event, I should not have expected a solo trip to Italy years later to be an exception to past experiences. It was Fr. Maurice McNamee, a Jesuit at St. Louis University, who introduced me to Casa di Santa Brigida. He was a Professor of Art History and English. Regularly, he made trips to Rome for research and, of course, enjoyment. Often, he would stay at the guest house of the Bridgettine nuns. With their black veils and "hot-cross-bun" caps, they were a familiar sight around the Vatican. Their guesthouse is in the same building where St. Bridget of Sweden lived in the late 14th century. Guests can see the original rooms of St. Bridget and her daughter, St. Catherine, along with relics. To top it all off, Casa di Santa Brigida is situated on a grand square made famous, in part, by the Palazzo Farnese, a Renaissance palace designed for Alessandro Farnese, Pope Paul III. Several of the greatest architects of the 16th century participated in its completion, including Michelangelo.

On Fr. Mac's recommendation, I booked a single room at the casa for a week. After I arrived and looked around, it was clear that it must be a favorite haunt of visiting clergy. By chance, on my first day, I happened to meet a bishop who invited me to a simple Mass. Five or six of us gathered in a small room with our chairs circling the space. Following the reading of the gospel, the bishop encouraged us to offer our thoughts on the text. As I recall, I was the only one who spoke up—a true stereotypical loudmouthed American tourist, I suppose. At the end of Mass, the bishop told us that he would be away for a couple of days.

Later that morning, I went sightseeing. St. Peter's Basilica was just a short walk from the casa. When I came back, a young nun approached me before I could return to my room. "A couple came to our door and told us they had a reservation," she said, excited and gesturing rapidly like an orchestra conductor. She explained to the couple that the casa was fully booked and she saw no record of their reservation. "So, what could we do?" she told me. "We gave them your room." I was more than surprised; speechless would be more accurate. Then the young nun added cheerfully, "You can stay in the bishop's room because he is away." Having already cleared out my room and transferred my luggage to the bishop's room, she led me there. When she opened the door, I thought, "Wow, this is nicer than my other room!" After we exchanged a few words, she left.

The first thing I did was open a large wardrobe. The bishop's clothes were still hanging there, which I thought was strange. Even so, I swung my suitcase on the bed and was ready to unpack. Suddenly, there was a knock on the door and an older nun entered. She was visibly agitated. "You cannot stay here," she said. "This is the bishop's room . . . no . . . no." Of course, I explained what the young nun told me. "Well, where can I stay?" I asked. "I had a reservation and my room was given away." Sister, now calmed down, told me that she had a nice room for me on another floor.

When we finally reached that destination, she opened a door to a large room, a library in fact, that also had a full-size piano in it. Sticking out like a sore thumb beside the piano was a fold-up bed. "Isn't this a beautiful room?" said Sister. "You'll be very comfortable here." After extolling more features of the room, she left. It did not take me long to realize that libraries, even those complete with pianos, do not come with toilets and showers. Later I learned that I had to walk down two or three flights of stairs to avail myself of both those facilities. Still, how often do you get to sleep overnight in a library in Rome on which there was not even a lock on the door? I am an avid reader but I never managed to find on the shelves any good books in English to curl up with. As for the piano, even "Chopsticks" was beyond my skill.

Fortunately, though, I have a good sense of humor, which Mark Twain, perhaps America's premier humorist, called the greatest blessing. Sleep that night did not come as easy as the laughter though. For the remainder of the week, the library was where I camped out. When the bishop whose room I occupied for a few brief minutes returned, he saw me in the dining hall. "Doris, I almost knocked on your door very early in the morning the other day," he said. He explained that he was going to Castel Gandolfo to see the pope and hoped to take me with him. "Oh, but I didn't want to wake you up or startle you when it was still dark outside," he said softly. Castel Gandolfo, of course, is the pope's summer home outside of Rome. I replied with a disappointed smile, "Oh, you could've knocked at 2 a.m. or 3 a.m. and I would've jumped out of bed raring to go." Well, I missed my best chance to personally meet a pope, John Paul II. However, I had a good story of "Roma" and "la dolce vita" nun-style!

Come to think of it, that story did have an encore. One of the nuns gave me a ticket to attend a weekly audience of the pope at Paul VI Hall just to the left of St. Peter's Basilica. The nun advised me to sit near the inner aisle because the pope might pass that way as he walked to the papal throne on the stage. Sometimes, she said, he even shook extended hands. For some reason, I decided the odds of that happening to me in a hall accommodating about 6000 people were slim, so I opted for a quick exit. My seat was directly on the outer aisle near one of the entrance doors, but still within very close view of the stage. When the pope did pass by, he and six excited people were to my left. Consequently, there was no papal handshake and eye contact for me, but that did not detract from the joy of being present!

6

EGYPT AND ISRAEL

From 1981 to late 1987, I worked in the international section of McDonnell Douglas Health Systems Division. My assignments took me to Australia, New Zealand, South Africa, England, Ireland, Canada, and other destinations. Those company travels came to a screeching halt when I was transferred to another division pursuing a major US military contract for computerized health systems. When the contract did not materialize, there was a layoff.

The predictable response to losing a job would be to hunker down and find another one. For some reason, I decided instead to take a trip to Egypt and Israel the following March. Easter that year was on April 3. I planned to end my trip in the Old City of Jerusalem, a walled area that encompasses the holiest places in Christianity, Judaism, and Islam. I suspected it would be a once in a lifetime adventure. Had I been following the nightly news more closely, perhaps I would have hesitated, but likely not.

Despite a peace treaty brokered between Egypt and Israel in 1979, their relationship was steadily chilling.[9] Moreover, the first

---

[9] On 26 March 1979, US President Jimmy Carter hosted the treaty between Israeli Prime Minister Menachem Begin and Egyptian President Anwar Sadat at the White House. It was the first peace treaty ever entered into by Israel and an Arab country.

Palestinian Intifada began in early December 1987, just about three months before my scheduled trip. Ongoing violence between the Palestinians and the Israelis would continue for more than five years. All in all, I was not headed for a fun in the sun vacation.

Normally, I traveled alone. In my family, I was the only one with wanderlust. On one occasion, I did manage to convince my mother and sister to take a trip to Ireland, where my maternal grandparents were born. For the most part, though, my international trips have been solo, often with land reservations and itineraries made on the fly. In this case, I exercised a modicum of common sense and decided to book a tour that included my chosen destinations.

It is strange what clings to your memory as time quickly passes. In Cairo, it is not the museums and artifacts, interesting though they were. I remember riding on a bus in slow, erratic traffic. A donkey cart had come to an incline. The back of the cart was stacked high with old furniture and other things. At the front of the cart was an old man, slumped to the outside. It was impossible to know if he was sleeping or in distress. A young boy sat beside him and held the reins to the donkey. The boy was beating the donkey with a whip. The donkey fell to its knees and could not get up. His rear end collapsed as well and he was lying in the street. The boy kept beating the donkey and yelling in Arabic. It was sickening to watch. I wanted to make it all stop and knew that I was helpless under the circumstances. The fury in the boy's face was so disturbing. The donkey was exhausted, resigned, unmoving. Slowly our tour bus moved on. However, some images remain with you, even though you would choose to wipe them away.

Until I visited Cairo, I never realized how close some pyramids were to the city. From a tall building, you can see them in the distance. With the pollution arising from the city, they look faded from that perch, but a ten mile drive into the desert clears the air. There on the west bank of the Nile stands the Giza Complex, three well-preserved pyramids. Early archaeologists believed the pyramids were built as burial tombs for pharaohs, but some scientists today are not convinced. In any case, the Giza pyramids were built for the pharaohs: Khufu, Khafre, and Menkaure—in that order, father, son, and grandson. The Great Pyramid of Khufu is the oldest and largest of the three pyramids, going back at least 4500 years. Entry into each pyramid required a separate fee. Of course, I chose to put my money on the Great Pyramid, one of the Seven Wonders of the Ancient World.

There are three chambers in the Great Pyramid. One chamber is within the bedrock. The "Queen's Chamber" and the "King's Chamber" are higher up in the pyramid. Once inside the pyramid, visitors could climb steep steps to see one of the interior chambers. The passage leading up to the chamber was very tight. As people were going up the steps, others were coming down. In some spots, hugging the walls was the order of the day.

Because there was no air circulation, it was also very stuffy within the pyramid. As we were approaching the chamber, a guide said that no one should proceed if he or she were at all claustrophobic. I never had any reason to suspect that I was, so I kept climbing. Then the guide said that to enter the chamber you had to bend very low to get through the opening. I asked a visitor who was on the way down the steps just how low was low. "You have to bend in half," he said. Then he added, "There is nothing inside the chamber at all, not even paintings on the wall." Suddenly, I was feeling claustrophobic and did a U-turn! Later I learned that the chamber was not even suspected as Khufu's resting place. Khufu's sarcophagus was never found anywhere in the pyramid. So, I did not feel that I had missed anything, except perhaps a strained back.

While some of our group proceeded upward, I proceeded downward and outward to look at the camels. As I was admiring a particular camel reclining on the sand, a young man asked if I would like to ride it. "No, thank you," I said. "Are you sure?" the young man asked. "He is a gentle camel and his name is Michael Jackson?" Of course, I had to laugh. "No, thank you," I replied. "But, will you take my picture by the camel?" When those words were spoken, I handed over my camera and stood at a sociable distance from the camel. The young handler raised the camera and took a picture. "Why don't you get closer to the camel?" OK. "No, move a little closer." OK. Some noise came from the camel's moving lips. "Why don't you just sit on the camel?" Cautiously, I replied, "O-o-k, but make sure Michael Jackson doesn't move!" As soon as I sat in the saddle, the handler pulled on a rope that had tethered the camel's feet. The back of the camel went up, and I thought I was going to tumble over his head. Then the front of the camel came up, and I thought I was going to slide off his rear. "Get me off this camel!" I shouted. "Oh, you'll love riding on the camel," the handler said. "We'll go around the pyramids." That is how I rode a camel in the desert; not quite like Lawrence of Arabia, but I did hang on. I wonder if Lawrence's camel had as famous a name as Michael Jackson?

In Egypt, our tour also visited Luxor Temple, about 400 miles south of Cairo. When we arrived, it was approaching twilight, so our time inside this amazing structure was limited. Under Amenhotep III, Ramses II, Tutankhamun, and other pharaohs, this largest temple in ancient Egypt took shape. As I wandered around, I eventually heard our tour guide's voice on a megaphone telling us to be back at the bus in five minutes. Admittedly, I tried to stretch out the deadline just a little bit longer, but then walked out the front entrance. Of course, I was not prepared for what I saw—no tour buses, no cars, no people. By now it was also dark. Only the lights from the temple grounds illuminated the surroundings. I just stood there, not knowing exactly what to do next. There were no smart phones or flip phones in 1988. Even if there were, I had no one to call. The thought of possibly spending the night in the temple briefly occurred to me. That would mean more time to explore the immense carvings, but who knew what night creatures might also be using this ancient shrine for shelter or how cold it might get at night?

Then I spotted a vehicle at the far end of the parking area. It was black and large. I stared at it for quite a while, not sure if I should start walking toward it. Before I could decide, the car slowly began heading my way. When it stopped near me, the driver got out of the car. He was wearing a long white robe and a head covering, traditional Arabic attire in the Middle East. A passenger in the front seat of the car was similarly dressed. The driver asked me why I was there alone. I explained the situation and he offered to take me to my hotel. He opened the passenger door and told his companion to move over to the driver's seat. Then he told me to get in the middle of the front seat. I smiled and said I would prefer to sit by the door. He said I would be more comfortable in the middle, but I repeated my preference. At that point, he got in the car, which sat very high. At 5 ft. 5 in., I boosted myself up—with some effort—and shut the car door.

As we were driving to the hotel, the man seated by me turned on an overhead light, took out a box, and opened it. Inside, was jewelry—rings, necklaces, and bracelets. He took one in his hand, held it up, and then passed it to me. I told him it was beautiful. As he continued to show me the jewelry and we drew closer to the hotel, he asked me if I would take him into my hotel so we could have dinner together. Politely, I thanked him for the ride. Then I said that it was late; when I reached my hotel, I was going straight to my room. He then said that I could at least take him into the hotel for a cup of coffee. Again, I thanked him but declined his suggestion. At that point, he said very slowly, "Do you understand what I am asking you?" I repeated what I had said earlier, including my gratitude for the ride. He turned to the driver and said with a clear tone of disdain, "Let her off here." When the car stopped, I slid out and the men quickly drove away.

Crossing the busy street and walking the short distance to the hotel, it occurred to me that I had offended the man, although I was not certain why. Perhaps a "thank you" was not sufficient and it was an insult not to repay his assistance, at least with a cup of coffee—which, coincidentally, I never drink. At its best, traveling to other countries is not just about seeing sites or wildlife, but learning how human beings are both alike and different because of their environment, history, and culture. Travel was an adventure, yes, but also an education. That night I was given a lesson and a rebuke.

In any event, when I entered the hotel and passed the dining room, I saw all the people from the tour. As I walked into the room, the tour guide came up to me and said, "We were wondering why you didn't come to dinner?" After I explained to him what happened at the temple, he was surprised and a bit embarrassed. Then he remembered that as the tour bus was getting ready to leave, someone came up and asked for a ride back to the city. Later, when they did the headcount, it matched the number written down on the manifest, so they drove away. On reflection, I thought my outcome could have been very different. So often in my life, I have felt that my guardian angel must be putting in overtime on my behalf. On the other hand, some family and friends believe I am missing a certain fear gene or perhaps have an abundance of trust genes! Are there such things?

Eventually, our tour started the "exodus" across the desert to Israel. I do remember passing an interesting monastery high up on a hill but I do not know its name. It seemed the only way to visit it would be to scale the sheer rock walls or find the path that was hidden from our eyes. Unfortunately for us but fortunately for the monks, tourists were not allowed. I suspect these spiritual descendants of the early Desert Fathers, like St. Anthony of Egypt, would not have found our chatter interesting or welcome.

Before going to Israel, we visited Petra in Jordan. To reach the ancient temple, Al-Khazneh, you walk about three-quarters of a mile through a high, winding, narrow gorge. Just when you think the gorge must go on as long as the Grand Canyon, you see a slit and then just a sliver of a building. As you round the narrow opening, the full temple comes into view. A dusty rose color, it was carved directly into a towering sandstone hill over 2000 years ago. Within the temple are hewn rooms, sometimes with marbled red ceilings. Beyond the temple are tombs and dwellings—even a Roman amphitheater—all carved from the multi-colored sandstone. Petra is considered one of the Seven Wonders of the Modern World.[10]

By the time our tour reached Tel Aviv, it was nearing Holy Week. Over the next few days, we visited many places: the Shrine of the Book, a repository for the Dead Sea Scrolls; the Church of the Nativity in Bethlehem, housing a grotto or cave that is venerated as the birthplace of Jesus; a first-century house in Nazareth, possibly like the childhood home of Jesus; and churches in Galilee that may approximate the locations where Jesus gave his Sermon on the Mount and multiplied a few fish to feed the hungry crowds. Toward the end of the tour, we headed south. On that drive, we saw the caves of Qumran where the Dead Sea Scrolls were discovered in 1947 by three Bedouin shepherds.[11]

The final destination of our trip was Masada. We approached it from the eastern side on a road that winds down the coast. About three decades before the birth of Jesus, King Herod the Great built a palace complex on a rock plateau at the edge of the Judean Desert and overlooking the Dead Sea. Jewish Zealots took shelter there after the destruction of Jerusalem in 70 AD. Roman soldiers sieged Masada in 73 AD. Its inhabitants—men, women, and children—were either killed by the Romans, starved to death, or committed suicide. The

---

[10] Shortly before the COVID pandemic reached the US, I was taking Brother Giovanni, a Hungarian vizsla, for regular visits to Mother of Good Counsel Home. As we walked the halls and saw a group gathered in the library, I peeked in. A young Sister of St. Francis of the Martyr St. George (quite a mouthful!) had gathered some of the residents there for entertainment and stimulation. She had a picture of the Great Temple at Petra on the table. Out of the blue, I said, "Oh, I've been there!" Sister asked me to talk to the group about it. Who knew my stopover in Petra would ever come in handy? Of course, my stumbling description could not compete with Gio's simple presence and encouraging nudges with his nose. He had the audience in the palm of his paw. Partnering with Gio has been a valuable lesson in humility. The last chapter of this book explores some of our adventures.

[11] These were the only authenticated fragments for sixty years. Just recently, though, more biblical fragments have been uncovered from a cave in the Judean Desert. The archaeological project that started in 2017 has also brought to light a mummified child from 6000 years ago and a basket that may be over 10,000 years old. That fascinating news did not escape my notice as I was writing my own "ancient" tale!

archaeologists and historians still do not have a definitive conclusion about the bodies that were uncovered.

To reach the top, visitors usually take a cable car. There is a Snake Path, but the name alone kind of saps your incentive. At 1300 feet, there is a beautiful panoramic view of the Dead Sea. Walking among the ruins of this ancient battle and thinking of the chaos and carnage that took place was both fascinating and solemn. Strange, though, how emotions and concentration can change very quickly on a tour. When we descended from the plateau, we drove to the shores of the Dead Sea. There was time to swim or just wade in the water. Even those who could not swim, quickly found out that the salt water would keep them afloat, like a bobbing cork. Thoughts of battles were put away, drowned in the sparkling water.

When the tour portion of my trip came to an end, I stayed in Jerusalem. During Holy Week, my guest house was right outside the Old City. I recalled its name was Notre Dame, because, at the time, I wondered if it was connected to Notre Dame University in the US or if it was an American guest house. A parochial American assumption! A quick search on the Web shows its full name, which I had forgotten: Notre Dame–Pontifical Institute of Jerusalem. When I clicked on a link and saw the photo of a large stone chapel, memories of praying there late at night flooded in from over thirty years ago. In the US, many Catholic churches are locked by 5 p.m., so there is no opportunity for late-night prayer before the tabernacle. The chapel was open around the clock. There was plenty of reason to pray in the darkness.

From my room at Notre Dame, I could hear gunshots at night, and guests were advised not to venture out. The escalating unrest between 1978 and 1988 resulted from the increasing settlement of Jews in the Muslim Quarter of the Old City that for forty years had none. It was reported that Ariel Sharon, who had once been Israel's Minister of Defense, had taken an apartment in the Muslim Quarter just three months earlier. For Muslims that was not exactly like having Mr. Rogers as their neighbor![12]

As I ventured into the Old City for the first time, I noticed there were very few tourists. To me, that was a plus because I could see all the holy sites without crowds. Gradually I came to understand that there were small crowds because there was an increased risk. In the daylight hours, though, I roamed the Old City on my own. An entrance was just a few steps away from the guest house.

One of the first places I visited was the Western Wall or Wailing Wall. It is the only remaining part of the Second Temple of Jerusalem which stood from 516 BC until 70 AD. At that point, it was destroyed by the Romans. That was about forty years after the death of Jesus. Likely, Jesus stood at one time before the Wailing Wall, spoke in the open square, or prayed in the temple. Like many visitors, I left a prayer on a tiny piece of paper stuffed into the crevice of the wall. It is not an ancient practice, more like a few hundred years old. Where else do you get to send God a written note? If you used the US mail, it would probably get mixed in with the Santa Claus letters. Supposedly, the notes at the wall are collected twice a year and buried at the Mount of Olives in the Jewish cemetery—a unique "Dead Letter Office" indeed!

Next to the Western Wall is the Dome of the Rock, a site important to Jews, Muslims, and Christians. Jews believe that Abraham came there to sacrifice his son, Isaac. Later, Solomon's Temple (the First Temple) was built at the site. Devout Muslims believe their Prophet Mohammed flew on his winged horse, al-Burāq, from Mecca to the Temple Mount, and then ascended to heaven. A dome was constructed as an Islamic shrine in the 7th century. Eventually, it

---

[12] *Mister Rogers Neighborhood* was a popular children's program in the US from 1968 to 2001. Fred Rogers, an ordained Presbyterian minister, was the host. The inhabitants of his Neighborhood of Make-Believe included puppets, like Daniel Tiger, Lady Elaine, Henrietta Pussy Cat, King Friday X111, and Donkey Hodie. The program always opened with a song: *Won't You Be My Neighbor?* Rogers died in 2003. The spin-off, *Daniel Tiger's Neighborhood* on PBS, carries on Roger's vision and gentleness.

collapsed, was rebuilt, captured by the Crusaders in the 12ᵗʰ century, and used as a Catholic church.

By the late 12ᵗʰ century, Muslims had recaptured the shrine in this religious tug-of-war. To enter the building, you must remove your shoes. While there were shoes scattered close to the entrance, I simply carried mine in. What do you do if someone accidentally walks off with your shoes? Unlike Christian churches, there are no images inside the dome, but there are beautiful geometric and swirling designs. The rock itself is huge. It would be difficult to calculate all the blood that has been shed and the lives that have been lost to claim it and protect it.

On Holy Thursday, I visited Gethsemane, the garden by the Mount of Olives, where Jesus was arrested the night before his crucifixion. Also, I went to Mass at Dominus Flevit (Jesus wept), a Franciscan church on the Mount of Olives with a large window looking out on the Dome of the Rock. As you attend Mass, you can see behind the priest at the altar the Old City spread out before you.

Then, on Good Friday, I walked the Via Dolorosa, which tradition says is the path Jesus walked on the way to his crucifixion. The first half of the Via Dolorosa runs through the Muslim Quarter. There were very few tourists gathered for the walk. At certain points along the way, there were small groups of people angrily shouting at us, sometimes with fists raised. I remember thinking that this was too much like the first Good Friday!

The Church of the Holy Sepulchre is in the Christian Quarter. Inside the church is a stairway leading up to what is believed to be the place of Jesus' crucifixion. Beneath glass and adjacent to an altar is a huge rock, which tradition says is Calvary or Golgotha. The rock extends below the floor level. Surrounding the visible portion of the rock is a room with an abundance of icons, statues, candles, gold, and silver.

At another part of the church is what tradition says is the tomb of Jesus. It is housed within an architectural shrine resembling a small building. With so few visitors, I was fortunate to be able to quickly enter and spend time at the tomb alone except for one of the orthodox priests watching the entrance. The room was small and there was something that resembled a plain marble sarcophagus built into the wall. That is not the tomb of Jesus. What is below the marble slab atop the sarcophagus may be the site of the tomb. Perhaps science can determine that what lies below—rock or earth or a carved stone—dates from the time of Jesus. Ultimately, though, for the Christian, faith is in the person of Jesus, not in even the most venerated sites.

When I returned to the guest house, it was dinner time so I went to the dining room. After checking the evening specials, I ordered dinner. Later the waiter asked me how I was enjoying my steak. I said it was delicious. As I told him where I had visited during the day, it was like a rock dropped on my head, and I said out loud, "Holy Cow!" Not that there was anything holy about the slice of the cow I had just finished off for dinner. On one of the most sacred days in the Christian calendar—Good Friday—and having earlier visited the rock of Calvary and the tomb of Jesus, I was eating meat for dinner. Catholics at that time did not eat meat on any Friday and here I was eating meat on Good Friday in the Holy Land. No excuse. No explanation. No incrimination. Still, it boggles the mind!

The final place I visited before heading home was Tel Megiddo in the Jezreel Valley. The Book of Revelation says this is where there will be a final battle between the forces of light and the forces of darkness: Armageddon. Since I did not have a car, I asked someone at the guest house to help me hire a driver. Not surprisingly, he was Jewish. It was about an 80-mile drive to Tel Megiddo. We talked of many things along the way—political and personal. Once we arrived at our destination, there were history lessons, as well. Interestingly, the first recorded battle in history occurred at Tel Megiddo in 1457 BC when the Egyptians defeated the Canaanites at the Battle of Megiddo. Perhaps there were earlier battles but this was the first in which we have written details about the weapons, the body count, and the outcome. Unfortunately, over the centuries there have been many more wars at Tel Megiddo and around the world. In my lifetime, the world's wars have been the deadliest. As for Megiddo, it was a city that was engineered for war, at least as far back as King Solomon. Strangely, when we arrived at Tel Megiddo, we were the only visitors. There was time to slowly walk amidst the ruins and time to ponder. I still remember what my Jewish companion said to me. "Doris, if your Jesus does come back at the end of time, he'll look first in Jerusalem for a rabbi because he won't understand what your priest is saying." I laughed. We laughed. At least there would be no fighting that day at Megiddo!

7

OKAVANGO DELTA

While living and working in South Africa, I made a trip to Botswana to visit Okavango Delta. The largest inland delta in the world, it is created by the Okavango River seasonally spilling into the Kalahari Desert. The safari camp where I planned to stay could not be accessed by road but only by a small airplane that took off from, at that time, an equally small village.

As it turned out, I was the only passenger on a two-seater plane, sitting so close to the pilot that our shoulders rubbed. To my surprise, he landed the plane literally out in the bush with no person in sight much less a camp. Instead, in sight were wildebeests near a rivulet. I might stand eye-to-eye with one of the youngsters but not with the adults. Adult wildebeests weigh 600 pounds or more and come equipped with curved horns.

Naturally, I was surprised when the pilot told me to exit the plane. He said that someone from the camp would pick me up. I opened the plane door and cautiously slide out. By the time my feet touched down, the pilot was already nearby, putting my luggage on the ground. When he started to climb back into the plane, I said, "Are you going to wait until the people from the camp come to get me?" He replied that he had to keep on schedule because he was delivering the mail. Even in Botswana, the mail must go through! With that expla-nation, he closed the plane door, started the engine, and away he flew.

For a while, I admired the wildebeests, but I became a little con-cerned as they started to move closer toward me. I moved a few paces away. Eventually, out of nowhere, a truck came along with two men in the cab. Assuming they were from my camp, I threw my luggage in the back of the truck and climbed in after it. There was no room for me anywhere else. Behind the cab of the truck, was a black chest-high bar. I held onto that bar as the truck drove away.

What I clearly remember from that drive was how hard it was to stay vertical and, of course, the elephants. We drove through what only could be called an elephant parade. On every side of the truck going one way were elephants going the other way. I was too thrilled by the sight to be afraid. If I could have wrested my grip from the bar, I think I would have reached out and touched one of those ele-phants. Because the land was so rugged and over-hanging branches were sometimes in our path, I kept gripping that bar and doing deep dips like an exercising ballerina, not that there is anything remotely ballerina-like about me.

When the elephants had finally passed, the driver stopped the truck, jumped out, and came around to the back where I was still hanging onto the bar and trying to steady my legs. I will never forget how he looked up at me and said, with disbelief, "Who are you?" Of course, I said, "Are you the guys from the camp that were supposed to pick me up?" His answer was swift and loud, "NO!" Fortunately, when I told him the name of the camp, he knew its location and said he could take me there. "You were very lucky," he said. "In that spot where you were waiting, there was a lion kill yesterday." Maybe that is why he let me swiftly board the truck—uninvited and unannounced. I never asked.

When I finally arrived at the camp, I did ask someone in charge why I was never picked up. I was told that things were hectic, and they lost track of time. God bless those two men in a truck! There were only a few people at the camp. The small tent that I was assigned was on the outer edges. I remember in the morning asking the tour guide, "What were those pigs that kept circling my tent last night?" For emphasis, I made snorting noises—just like I had harmonized from my tent the night before. The tour guide walked me to my tent and finally answered. "Those weren't pigs," he said. "They were hippos." He showed me the tracks circling my tent. From all the nature programs I had watched, I knew that hippos kill more people than any other animal in Africa, so that was sobering. I like to think my snorting noises convinced the hippos that I was one of them!

The next day or so, we rode a small boat to a different area of the delta. When we climbed out of the boat, we sat on some fallen tree trunks to have our lunch. For some reason that I cannot explain (maybe because I was the youngest person there and by myself), one of the guides motioned from the trees for me to come to him and put his finger over his lips. He was a Tswana, one of the Bantu-speaking people of the delta. While the others were still eating and talking, I walked toward the guide. He did not speak but just motioned for me to follow him into the bush. When he finally stopped, I stopped. Slowly raising his hand, he pointed a few yards ahead of us where an elephant was browsing on tree leaves and twigs. Then, touching his nose and shaking his head left to right, the guide seemed to be telling me that the elephant could not smell us because we were upwind. As soon as the elephant started to flap its ears, the guide motioned that we had to leave. When we returned to the other tourists, neither of us mentioned what we had seen. Likely, they had not noticed we were gone. It was a gift and trust that the Tswana guide gave me, for what reason I will never know. What I do know is that it was a blessing!

8

GALAPAGOS ISLANDS

In late May of 2021, there was a news story about a female giant tortoise that had been found in 2019 on Fernandina Island in the Galapagos. The last confirmed sighting of that species was in 1906. A sample was taken from the 100-year-old tortoise, named Fern, to compare with the stored remains of a male. Scientists at Yale University announced a genetic similarity. Fern belonged to the species Chelonioids phantasticus, roughly "tortoise illusion." What an interesting name! Now the focus is on finding a male tortoise on Fernandina to save a species from extinction.

That news story brought back memories, not quite as far back as Fern's. The Galapagos Islands are part of the Republic of Ecuador and are located about 850 miles off the west coast of South America. The first reference to any visitor was that of a Dominican bishop from Panama, Tomas de Berlanga, who ended up in the Galapagos Islands in 1535 when the wind swept him off course while sailing to Peru. By 1570 the Galapagos were on the map—or a map . . . somewhere.

Their most famous visitor came much later. Charles Darwin was only twenty-two when he made his first trip there on the HMS Beagle in 1835. He spent five weeks taking notes on birds, tortoises, iguanas, penguins, blue-footed boobies, wild-flowers, volcanoes, and much more. Darwin made the Galapagos famous, first in the scientific community and then beyond through his book, *On the Origin of Species* (1859). While scientists made trips to the Galapagos, tourists began coming around in 1934, when there were an estimated 200 visitors. When I traveled there in the early 1970s, there were approximately 6000 visitors a year. Now their numbers are in the hundreds of thousands.

As I recall, my trip to the Galapagos was my first venture outside North America. At the time, I was living in Florida—young and eager to see as much of the world as I could. Also young was the man who organized the trip. He had a company with one employee, himself. I remember him carrying the passenger luggage as we moved about and covering all the bases that needed to be covered. There were only a few of us adventurers—maybe ten, I guess—who boarded the passenger ship. We slept and ate on the ship, going from island to island. At sea, most of our time was on the rear deck, taking in the sunshine, the sea air, the sea creatures, and at the appropriate times breakfast, lunch, and dinner. Somewhere in my photos—I will need to dig deep one day—there are pictures from that trip. One shows me standing on a beach in cutoff shorts with my back to the water when a Galapagos sea lion came from behind and pressed his nose and whiskers on my leg. A fellow passenger had his camera raised and was laughing. I did not know why until I felt that greeting from this beautiful sea creature. The sea lion had no fear of me, and I had no fear of him. There was something Eden about it all.

However, Eden had a short run, as the bible tells us. Later there was a baby penguin alone and stressed on the beach. When I pointed it out, I was told that no one could interfere. The animals had to be left to their fate—unless you were a rare giant tortoise. Though, even then, nature was a formidable opponent against the scientists. Lonesome George, a Pinta Island tortoise, died in 2012, apparently the last of his species. I also remember walking down a steep hill and finding at the bottom some giant tortoises. Stupidly, I gently sat sideways on one of the giants for a photo. This is why tourists cannot be trusted with the wildlife!

Fortunately, I did not crack his shell. Male tortoises can weigh 600 pounds and their honey-combed shell is very hard. In my case, I quickly stood up as the tortoise began to walk away with me. As for our journey up the hill, the thick vines and undergrowth made it much more arduous. To me, though, everything about the Galapagos was beautiful, even the barren landscapes, stretching out from volcanoes, cragged and red.

The trip was notable, also, for an acquaintance I made among the passengers, quite incidentally. Once in a while, we happened to be on the stern of the boat, enjoying the ocean scenery at the same time. She was soft-spoken. Soon others would gather around to join the conversation, as one would expect on a small ship. I was not even certain what the woman's name was. All I knew was that she was a nice older lady who was there with her daughter, Lucy, and her son-in-law, Rod. Eventually, one of the male passengers asked if I knew who she was. I replied, "No." He lowered his voice, "Elizabeth Dos Passos." I did not register any surprise so the man whispered, "She's the wife of John Dos Passos." Even that did not immediately ring a bell. After a long pause, I said, "Do you mean the writer, John Dos Passos?" He nodded.

John Dos Passos, of course, was a major American author. At least for a while, he also was a friend of Ernest Hemingway. They met in Spain and later, during the First World War, volunteered as ambulance drivers, retrieving the dead and wounded from the front lines. After the war, they both wrote about some of their experiences. Hemmingway died in 1961 and Dos Passos in 1970.

After that trip, Betty, as she liked to be called, and I exchanged a few letters, including when I moved to New Zealand in 1978. I had asked her if she ever met Graham Greene. In one of her letters that I came across recently, she said she had wanted to meet him but he told her that he was too old to make the trip now from his home on the French Riviera. Betty wrote about going to her old college, Longwood in Farmville, Virginia. It was founded in 1839, making it one of the oldest universities in the US. The speaker on that occasion, Betty said, was Virginia Carr, who was writing a biography of her husband.[13]

After returning to the US, I happened to be on a business trip to Washington DC and phoned Betty just to say hello. To my surprise, she invited me to the family home at Spence's Point, 100 miles south of Washington DC. It had been declared a National Historic Landmark in 1971. The drive along the Potomac was very pleasant. That afternoon Betty and I talked, and she graciously showed me around her home, including her husband's office. Later we had dinner and I spent the night. It was the last time I saw her.

Recently, a friend of mine, Loretta Dolan, told me I should write down the story of my life. She said she had written down her own story for her children and grandchildren. I told her that I did not want to do that. What I wanted to do was write about the places that I have seen and the people I have met. That is where grace shines, even in memory.

---

[13] *Dos Passos: A Life* (Virginia Carr, New York: Doubleday, 1984).

9

KENYA

Many years ago, in 1995 according to an expired passport, I was invited to Kenya by a Jesuit priest that I had met at St. Louis University, Otieno Ndongo. During his stay in the United States, I had taken him to various sites and he kindly offered to do the same for me in Kenya.

When I arrived at the Jesuit residence in Nairobi, Otieno showed me around. The residence was built around a central courtyard. The provincial, an American as I recall, had a dog that bounded across the courtyard to greet me. Consequently, I was first introduced to the dog and then to his master. The latter invited me to dine with his Jesuit companions. I was both surprised and delighted at the food. When I voiced this observation, one of the Jesuits reminded me, with a smile, that his order is not known for ascetics. After the meal, Otieno broke the news to me that, as a woman, I could not stay at the Jesuit house. The provincial decided that I could lodge in the Jesuit Refugee Office. Presumably, I became an American refugee, of sorts.

As one might expect, the Jesuit Refugee Office looked like a no-frills, low-maintenance operation. Otieno led me to a small room on the upper floor. Against the far wall was a cot. It was approaching evening and still very hot both in the room and outside. There was no air conditioning and no fan, so Otieno opened a window by my cot and wished me a good night's sleep. Unfortunately, the sleep fairy missed that communication. What prevented my sleep was not just the evening heat but the mosquitos that were enjoying a pool of water directly below my window. The females were very likely laying eggs as water is often a mosquito nursery. Afterward, some of the mosquitos flew up and through the window for an evening snack, and I was on the menu.

By the morning, I was not only yawning but covered with mosquito bites. When Otieno came by to take me to breakfast, he was surprised to see the bites. Back at the Jesuit residence, Otieno took me to see Angelo D'Agostino, a Jesuit priest and a medical doctor. Dag, as he was called, was immediately concerned about the mosquito bites, especially because of the prevalence of malaria in Nairobi and other parts of Kenya. He gave me some medication. Then he told Otieno to go out immediately and buy me a mosquito net for my room.

When we were alone, Dag said that he wanted to take me on a drive without Otieno. The Jesuits had acquired five acres of land on which he planned to build a health clinic, a school, and a cemetery for children with HIV. We went to see the land. It was all overgrown with tall grass and plants. The only building on the grounds had broken windows. Inside were leaves, tree limbs, and lots of dirt. I helped Dag sweep out some of the debris. Later, Dag took me outside and showed me the plot that would be the cemetery. At that time, contracting HIV was generally a death sentence. In my mind, I could visualize the simple wooden crosses that someday would stretch out further and further in what was now tangled grass and fallen branches.

Returning to the building, Dag picked up an old computer that had belonged to USAID, the US Agency for International Development. He had not been able to start it. Because I worked in the computer field, he handed it over to me. With persistence, I managed to get it booted, but I told Dag that it would likely be useless for what he wanted, which was to track medical and patient data. At that time, he also asked me if I could find out whether there were HIV drugs in St. Louis that could be sent to him for the children.

When I returned to St. Louis, I did approach the research hospitals in the city to ask about current and experimental drugs for HIV and whether I could send them to Kenya for children dying from the disease. The researchers all said that was not possible. The approved drugs in the US were very expensive and only prescribed for adults. I always felt I failed Dag in that endeavor but nothing stopped him from turning his dream into reality. The dream was Nyumbani, Swahili for home—a home for children with HIV.

Alongside Dag on that journey was Sr. Mary Owens. One Sunday, I met Dag outside a nearby church where he was celebrating Mass. He introduced me to Sr. Mary Owens. When Dag died in 2006, she continued the leadership of Nyumbani. Responding to one of my emails almost ten years later, she put me in touch with Dag's brother, Joe. He lived with his wife, Mary Ellen, in Richmond, Virginia. Joe was very active in supporting Dag in the US, including organizing benefit dinners for Nyumbani in the Washington DC area. These gatherings attracted some members of the US Congress. Also, Dr. Anthony Fauci, a familiar face to Americans because of COVID-19, was a personal friend and supporter of Dag. Through email exchanges with Joe, I met another member of the D'Agostino family, Anthony, who, at the time, was the Director of the Criminal Justice Ministry in St. Louis. More recently, he is working with the homeless as the Director of St. Patrick Center.

Amazing, all that grace that came into my life started with mosquito bites and Dag's medical concern. Most people cannot help looking over their shoulder, questioning their decisions and the roads not taken. Certainly, I have when it comes to Nyumbani. Yet, my heart tells me that even though we may not follow the same path as those we admire, we are forever stamped with their goodness. Some are promoting the cause of sainthood for Dag. Perhaps Sr. Mary Owens, who retired at the end of 2021, will end up on that same track!

As well as adventures of the spirit, there were wildlife adventures on that trip to Kenya. On one, in particular, Otieno and another Jesuit signed out a community car and took me on a road trip to Tanzania. When we reached Arusha, I hired a safari vehicle with a sliding roof and a guide to drive us to Ngorongoro, about two hours away. Ngorongoro is a volcanic crater. Within the crater are about 25,000 animals, including the Big Five: rhino, elephant, lion, buffalo, and leopard. It seems as though many of the animals have their designated spots. Want to see elephants? They are over here. Want to see a rhino? They are over there. The leopard is more secretive; the lion is more brazen. In one case, the guide pulled alongside a slope and the two Jesuits were able to poke their heads out of the open roof and be eye-to-eye with a lion. Unfortunately, I was seated in the wrong place and on the wrong side for that close-up. From the front seat of the vehicle, I just caught a peek at the lion as we turned for more exploring. What an outstanding memory, though, for the two J's!

Ngorongoro Crater has been called "Africa's Garden of Eden." I suspect one reason is that the animals seem content to exist in their "ordained" space. Of course, that is a tourist's perception from a safari vehicle in daylight, not likely that of the impalas with eyes peeled, day and dusk, on the lions.

For some, the way to God is through loving and serving the poor and sick among us. For others, the surest way to God is through a wilderness, including one that is well cared for, watched over, but still inhabited by wild animals that never fail to be authentic.

When the safari ended, we drove back to Arusha, eventually in heavy rain. One clear memory of our arrival is stepping out of the vehicle and into water that was almost up to my knees. I was not singing in the rain, but I was sloshing and laughing in it!

10

ICELAND AND GREENLAND

My original plan was to fly to Belgium, rent a car, and visit Germany, France, Italy, and Austria. As it turned out, Icelandair had the cheapest flights. Of course, the first stop was Iceland, which is about 1300 miles from Belgium by air. So, I decided to take that route and skip the second leg of the flight for a few days. The rest of my plan was less than sketchy.

When my flight landed in Reykjavik, I had no hotel or car reservations and no itinerary. As I was in line waiting to depart the plane, I turned to the stewardess near the exit door. "Can you recommend a hotel for me?" I went on to explain that I had never been to her country before. A simple and perhaps naïve question! She told me to step aside and let the passengers behind me continue to exit the plane. When all the passengers had cleared the exit, the stewardess, clearly concerned, came and spoke to me. "My mother has a spare room," she said. "You would be welcome to stay there." Of course, I was surprised by that generosity and asked the stewardess if she was certain her mother would not mind. She assured me that I would be a welcome guest and asked me to wait for her while she finished her onboard duties.

We talked as she drove to her mother's home and she learned more about this strange American who was unexpectedly going to be part of her family for a few days. It was a bright, modern house and her mother showed me a lovely room. She could not have been more gracious. From my bedroom window, I could see a green trimmed field and beyond that a large building. The mother asked if I played chess and I said unfortunately I did not. I thought perhaps one of the family wanted to start a game. Instead, she told me the building that I was gazing at was Laugardalshöll, a sporting arena where Bobby Fisher became the first American to win the World Chess Championship. That was in 1972 when he defeated Boris Spassky, the Russian grandmaster. For chess enthusiasts, it was the Match of the Century.

As it turned out, I never went to visit the arena, even though it was just a short walk across the field. Of course, I had plenty of time to stare at it from my window. This was the season of the midnight sun in Iceland. Between May and July, sunlight is 24 hours a day. Even though I was getting to Reykjavik late in the evening and was tired from the long flight, outside my window was a bright sunny day, perfect for an afternoon picnic. Sleeping was a bit of a challenge, even with closed blinds. However, in the next few days, I did take advantage of all that sunlight to explore the natural wonders in the vicinity of Reykjavik, like geysers, lagoons, waterfalls, and miles of open space.

When I found out that there were flights from Iceland to Greenland, I decided to book one as well. Greenland is the largest island in the world and, at that time, was not much of a tourist attraction. I am not sure if it is today. Its population then was less than 50,000 and ninety percent of the inhabitants were Inuit, the indigenous people of the Arctic. Plus, about eighty percent of Greenland was covered by an ice sheet, the second largest one in the world. Antarctica has it beat! Generally, people live along the western coast in settlements or small villages. In any event, my efforts to book a flight to Greenland proved to be a nonstarter. Reservations were full and flights were only once a week. However, when I mentioned this to my stewardess/fairy godmother, she said that she would try to get me on a flight. Voilà, she succeeded! There was one last-minute cancellation.

Even though this journey was many years ago, there is one incident I have never forgotten. The pilot of Icelandair landed the small plane on an old airstrip. When the passengers disembarked, we began walking to an Inuit village on the coast. I had injured my knee before the trip to Iceland, so I was limping. As we walked, I started to lag behind and quickly found myself at the end of the line. From a distance, an Inuit woman, who was all alone on a small hill, motioned to me with her outstretched hand to come toward her. Without hesitation, I did.

As I drew near, smiling, she took my hand and, without a spoken word, guided me on a shorter, easier path to the village. The guide and other passengers marched on, apparently without any inkling that I was missing. Before they arrived, I was able to see, undisturbed, one of the most remote villages in Greenland. Men were sitting by the shore with nets; boats tied up; large ice chunks floating in the water, perhaps from melting icebergs; whale spouts and voices rising from the sea.

Of course, from the perspective of the villagers, my presence changed their dynamic. Soon the children approached with their hands clutching beautiful hand-carved animals made from whale's teeth and bone. The Inuit are hunters of polar bears and whales. On the plane, we were asked not to buy any of the artifacts from the children but rather from designated government shops. This was hard to do because the children, as you can imagine, were charming, not to mention good sales kids. Perhaps this policy was to discourage commercialism in the Inuit culture and keep it unchanged. The presence of tourists was the change. Before leaving Iceland, I did purchase a piece of Inuit art from one of those designated shops at the airport. That figure of a polar bear sits on my bookshelf today.

When I think about that trip, I wonder how it all came about. What are the chances that a stewardess would take me to her mother's home or that there would be only one cancellation for the flight to

Greenland? What should I make of the Inuit woman, who saw me limping, took me by the hand, and lead me on a gentler path? Some would say that it was all just chance or coincidence. Maybe it was. All I know is that I left myself open—to possibility, kindness, and grace—and that led to a joy-filled adventure!

CARVED POLAR BEAR

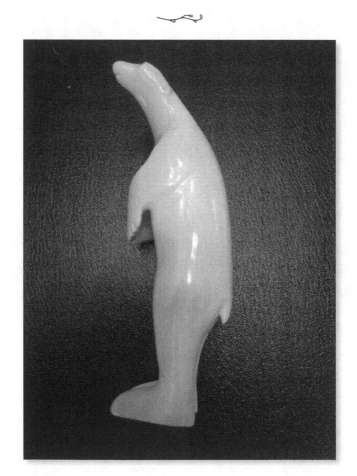

11

SOUTH AFRICAN JOURNAL

The Flights

I left St. Louis on 31 January 1996.[14] It was one of the coldest days of the winter. Mary Ann and Ron drove up that morning from Poplar Bluff. Diane was in and out of my house with some of her moving boxes and her moving pets. My cats, Kenya and Baby Ninja,

---

[14] This journal is about a point in time and a broad mission. Earlier, I made other travels to South Africa at different times, for different reasons, and resulting in different perspectives. From 1981 to 1987, I worked at McDonnell Douglas Health Systems in their international division. South Africa was one of the countries I visited. As a result, I experienced South Africa both before and after apartheid, a system of racial segregation and discrimination. On one of those earlier visits, I remember standing on Table Mountain and staring out at a little island in the distance, Robben Island, where Nelson Mandela was imprisoned for eighteen years, from 1964 to 1982. Altogether, he spent 27 years in prison, including Pollsmoor Maximum Security Prison (1982-1988) and Victor Vester Prison (1988-1990). My manager at McDonnell Douglas briefed me before sending me to South Africa. When I arrived, I understood the warnings about bomb threats in airports and buildings, heightened security, and travel restrictions. There was less time for friendships and exploration. The focus was on gathering information related to business goals and opportunities. On the contrary, a Fulbright Award promotes immersion, interaction, understanding, cooperation, and exploration. All those endeavors are reflected in the South African Journal.

were overwhelmed by the noise and fuss. One retreated under the bed and the other to the top shelf of the bedroom closet. I had to say goodbye to Kenya by leaning over the bed, spread-eagled, and reaching my hand between the bed and the wall. I searched until my hand felt soft fur and a rough tongue. To reach my brave (as in "discretion is the better part of valor") Baby Ninja, I boosted myself to the top shelf of the closet with a handhold on the clothes rod. One drawback of human evolution is that most of us left the grace and agility of the apes behind us, along with our long tails!

Mary Ann and Ron drove me, seven suitcases, and two carry-on bags (including my Macintosh PowerBook and printer) to the airport in their still new-smelling Pontiac. Ron had some concern about damaging the upholstery with the luggage, but apparently necessity overcame anxiety. At the airport, the TWA check-in agent charged me $429 for "excess luggage." This was a shock. In any event, I had two choices: pay or stay. Reluctantly, I chose the former.

On the way to the gate, I was asked to open my laptop's carrying case. At that point, I realized that I had left my laptop's power adapter still plugged into an extension cord at home. Mary Ann and Ron had to dash back there to get it. While I waited for them to return, Roland came by the gate. I had phoned him at his office at 6:30 that morning to say goodbye and gave him my departure gate, just in case he had time to come to the airport. Meanwhile, Mary Ann and Ron returned, so there were a few minutes for a final family reunion.

Roland stayed about twenty minutes and then had to leave for a 1:30 p.m. meeting. Mary Ann and Ron waited until I boarded the plane. Saying goodbye was hard. The TWA flight was supposed to be airborne at 1:15 p.m., but it was closer to 2:00 p.m. before its wheels left the ground. On board the flight, I was seated next to a young woman, Angie, who was on her way to Germany to spend a month with her parents. We chatted during the two-hour flight.

When I arrived at JFK Airport in New York, I had to catch a shuttle bus to another terminal. That carry-on luggage was beginning to feel like a ton of bricks. I was walking as fast as I could to the gate when I heard the announcement for my flight. Final boarding call! For me, though, this rushing was preferable to sitting and waiting in a terminal.

On the South African Airways flight, I sat in the small cabin upstairs. I had an aisle seat, and fortunately there was no one in the middle seat. At the window was Marie, a South African pensioner who had just been to the US to see her son and his family in Alabama. She was wearing a University of Alabama sweatshirt. Marie and I got on well. She lives in Pretoria (where Nelson Mandela serves as president of South Africa) and is a part-time tour guide.

My race to the departure gate turned out to be unnecessary. "Hurry up and wait," as the military expression goes. The plane sat on the tarmac for about an hour in New York, due to icy conditions and traffic. The actual flight to Johannesburg was good but long—almost fourteen hours. Our plane had some strong tailwinds, the pilot said, so the time was shorter than expected. The food on board was excellent by airline standards; better, I think, than any American carrier I have been on. The in-flight movie was an old British comedy that was not worth watching, especially since I was tired. So, I just tipped my seat back and tried to rest.

Arrival in Johannesburg

We arrived in Johannesburg at about 4 p.m. on February 1. I was supposed to connect with a flight to Durban at 5 p.m. Since I had to go through passport control first and the lines for "aliens" were very long, I was beginning to think I would not make it. However, the attendant at passport control assured me I would. With twenty minutes until liftoff, I collect my baggage off the conveyor belt that wound around like a sleeping python. All the other passengers and their carts were jammed around the belt. It was as though they were sunbathers protecting their two-foot-square beach plot. Finally, some of my bags began to arrive. More and more passengers were leaving, and I was still staring at the python, waiting for it to cough up the rest of my luggage.

Soon, I was the last person, and it was clear that one bag had been "digested." I reported it to the help desk attendants and abandoned all hope of ever seeing my suitcase—the largest one, of course—ever again. I also looked at my watch and realized my flight was probably leveling off. The flight attendants were serving drinks to the lucky passengers minus one. The help-desk attendants assured me everything would be okay, arranged another flight for me, and sent me off. As I wheeled my surviving suitcases through customs, no one was around. I could have smuggled in six bags of Intel chips, CDs, or plutonium and be living comfortably off my black-market booty by now!

I checked my bags at the South African Airlines desk for my flight to Durban. The ticket agents asked why I had paid $429 excess baggage charges in St. Louis. I told them that the TWA agent said he had to collect the money for South African Airlines; the amount was not negotiable. Was I supposed to go home, repack, and try again tomorrow? Tomorrow is another day, Scarlet? The sun will come out tomorrow, Annie? I do not think so! I did say that for $429 my bags deserved a seat on the plane. The SAA ticket agents agreed and at least commiserated with me over the seeming greed of American capitalism.

Anyway, with one bag missing and $429 squandered, I proceeded to the gate and waited for my 6 p.m. flight to Durban. Sitting next to me on the bench was a young American woman. She was in South Africa to spend time with her boyfriend. Excitedly, she gave me the scoop that on my flight from New York were several celebrities— Johnny Cochrane of the O.J. Simpson defense team; the TV actor Robert Guillaume; and the "son" from The Cosby Show. I did not see them. First-class passengers seemed to be whisked on and off with a cloaking device that rivals a Klingon starship. Here and there are only unconfirmed sightings. The flight to Durban was airborne on time, and I arrived one hour later at 7 p.m.

Arrival in Durban

At the baggage claim, I gathered up my remaining bags, like the shepherd gathering the sheep and mourning the loss of one. I think slinging those bags on the cart took almost as much effort as slinging a darted, inert sheep—that is how heavy they were. A couple of times, the suitcases slid from cart to floor and had to be persuaded back again.

When I walked through the glass doors and into the passenger-arrival area, I am sure I looked like a tired and sweaty sight. In the crowd were a man and a woman holding up a sign: Dr. Schoenhoff. Well, folks, the doctor is finally in! Professor Patricia Berjak[15] and her husband, Professor Norman Pammenter, had come to fetch me.

They drove me to my cottage right on the grounds of the University of Natal.[16] Norman and I carried in the suitcases, as well as the bags of groceries that he and Pat had bought for me. Mrs. Theo Baillache, the matron in charge of the university cottages, was there to open the door. She only stayed a few minutes. Pat and Norman asked if I would like to come to their house for dinner or just go to bed. Without hesitation, I chose the latter option. After Pat and Norman left, I spent the next hour or so unpacking luggage and putting things away on shelves. Then I took a cold shower (not intentionally) and went to bed. The bed was small; Grumpy, Sneezy, or Bashful might have found

---

[15] When I met Patricia Berjak, I did not realize that she was a world-renowned botanist known in her field for her work on plant seeds. One of her interests was cryobiology, the study of low temperatures on living things. Another was cryopreservation, the process of freezing cells and tissues to prevent the loss of genetic diversity on our planet. For example, the Millennium Seed Bank in Sussex, England stores two billion seeds gathered from 38,000 species. Pat was particularly interested in recalcitrant seeds that cannot survive extreme water loss and freezing. Her academic conferences took her well beyond South Africa, including China. Sometime after I had left South Africa, she and her husband attended a conference in St. Louis (MO), and we were able to enjoy each other's company once more. Pat died on 21 January 2015 at the age of 75.

[16] In January 2004, the University of Natal merged with the University of Durban-Westville to become the University of KwaZulu-Natal.

it comfortable, though. To me, it looked like an army or prison cot. It was a one-inch foam mattress on a metal frame. I was up several times that night with jet lag. There was also noise coming from the two nearby streets, Princess Alice and Francois.

Cottage at 352 Princess Avenue

The cottage at 352 Princess Alice Avenue had four rooms: bedroom, living room, dining room, and kitchen. It was probably built forty or fifty years ago, and the furniture was old and very basic. The only furniture that looked fairly new was a living room suite in pink Naugahyde. In the dining room was a small table with mismatched chairs, definitely not suitable for Mary Ann's Thanksgiving dinners! In the kitchen was a sink with no cabinet underneath, a stove, a new Defy refrigerator (a South African brand), and a small cupboard for dishes and can goods.

The bathroom was small. There was an old toilet with the "tank" way up high and a yank chain. A basin was directly under the window. The bathtub had a makeshift shower with a flexible extension and a removable showerhead. I quickly discovered that the water faucets were reversed for an American, i.e., red-tabbed faucets indicated cold water while blue-tabbed faucets indicated hot water. Well, I am in the Southern Hemisphere. The poles are reversed, so why not reverse the water faucets? In my house tour, I keep repeating small, small, small. I lack the imagination of a realtor.

Between both the front and back door and the outside world is a steel cage door with a padlock. On the inside door are a chain, a deadbolt, and two slide bolts—one at the top and one at the bottom. On all the large windows are security bars. This security is light by South African standards. You should see homes with brick walls, electronic alarms, guard dogs, and "armed response" signs. All of this is in addition to cage doors and window bars. Someone is expecting a revolution!

What tight security did not keep out were geckos, three-inch roaches, and hefty ants. I can understand how, in the ghettos, people said the rats became pets. I was beginning to talk to the geckos. One day I found a baby gecko in my bathroom basin. I was afraid he would go down the drain, so I tried to coax him onto a piece of white bond paper. Of course, he turned tail and went right down the drain. Then I started worrying that I had shortened the life of this baby gecko. I thought about a movie I had seen in which giant alligators were living in the sewers of New York. I could picture the African sequel: Giant Mutant Geckos from the Drains of Durban! I kept thinking about how I would get the gecko out, like lowering a tightly-rolled piece of paper towel so he could climb up. By the time I came back with my hook and ladder, as it were, the gecko was sitting in the basin again, looking up at me. Who said reptiles were low on the intelligence chain? Of course, if a gecko can climb upside down across a ceiling with those high traction feet, he can climb up a drain pipe. Put that in your Scout Handbook!

The cottage was fenced in and had a small backyard and front yard. I could not sit outside because ants were everywhere. Across my front yard, I also saw a monkey troop parading by one Sunday afternoon, the babies clinging tightly to the fur of their mother's belly. I spotted them in the trees each day as I climbed to work. That climb was a bit like walking from the bottom to the top of the hill at Grandpa Duff's home in Ironton. More than once, I thought about how physically fit Uncle Jay was to make that climb each day. As for me, I was like a panting dog by the time I reached my building each day. However, I made it, stopping for a few minutes halfway up to watch the monkeys in the tree canopy over my head.

I stayed in the cottage for one month. Mrs. Baillache and Pat Berjak thought I should move because I was not "safe." I finally agreed to move because I had no privacy in the cottage. It faced the main street, and I had to leave windows wide open since there was no air conditioning or fan. Because of the humidity in Durban, it can feel hotter than the temperature suggests. I was soaked every day with perspiration. Plus, as I moved around, especially at night, I might as well have been in a department store window modeling Woman's World lingerie.

On Sunday, after Mass, in the rain, with no one to help me, and walking uphill and down, uphill and down, I packed everything into my rental car (a Nissan Sentra) and moved. If I had known how exhausting it would be, I would have hired some students. It took me all morning, but I did it.

Shepstone Building: Flat A

The flat I am currently occupying is in a building that houses Computer Services, Architecture, and some workshops. There are only two flats in the building. I am in Flat A, and Theo Baillache is in Flat B. Many people, who have been at this university for years, do not even know these flats are here. Both apartments are side by side in one corner of the building's parking garage. Our parking spaces were right outside our apartment doors. Each parking space had a name tag, but the sign above mine said "Occupant Transit Flat." At first, I would come back after work and find a car in my space. Perhaps, the drivers thought that space was for people who were "coming and going." Even though that could well describe me, Mrs. Baillache had the maintenance department put up a sign—Dr. Schoenhoff, Reserved—to discourage people from parking there. That must have been a little more intimidating because the sign seems to be working.

Apart from the lack of privacy in the previous cottage, the main reason I wanted to move to the flat was that it has a balcony (about three floors up) that overlooks the hills of Natal and a small nature reserve. This reserve is where the monkeys sneak out and come onto the campus. I have a beautiful view of sunrises, and at night I can lie in bed and see the lights of Natal spread across the darkness. Also, my walk to the biology building is cut about in half. Some uphill climbing remains, but not nearly as steep.

One interesting aspect of my flat is that it has three refrigerators.

I may look like a big eater, but this is ridiculous. Hopefully, maintenance will come soon and haul away two of them. Mrs. Baillache suggested I use them for closet space, but I do not want to open a refrigerator to get my socks and underwear. That would give a whole new meaning to "shiver me timbers!" One refrigerator is brand new: the Defy. I had to remove the packing tape and set up the shelves. There is also a new microwave which I bought because I rarely cook a meal. Does egg on toast count? Mrs. Baillache surprised me, as well, with a new mattress for my double bed. Ah, no more gripping the sides of a cot!

Over the last few weeks, I have also bought some African art for the flat. My favorite piece is a hippo pool, complete with four hippos. The pool and hippos are all carved out of one piece of stone. The piece is about fourteen by eleven inches, and it is heavy. It is sitting on my coffee table and makes me smile just to see it. The cost was about $37. The hippo pool is from Zimbabwe, but I bought it in Umhlanga, a seaside area north of Durban. The woman who sold it said she had run the store for ten years and had never seen another one like it. It was tucked away on a bottom shelf, but it caught my eye immediately. All of thirty seconds later, I decided to buy it. I had the strange feeling that I had bought one like it before. It was as though I recognized it when I saw it. On my desk are two other pieces from Zimbabwe. In the foyer are two pieces "from up north." The store owner did not know their exact location. One of those pieces is signed on the bottom. Sitting on the cabinetry that surrounds my bathtub is a "swamp fairy." It depicts a sleeping hippo with white water lilies on its back and two green ferns sticking up like cherub wings. I just thought the pottery was whimsical.

At one time, my flat belonged to the caretaker of the building. A man, his wife, and his child used to live in a car parked right outside the entrance to the university. Some staff at the university felt sorry for them. They bought a tire for the car since one was hopelessly flat and unrepairable. Then they found the man a job as a caretaker at the university and set his family up in the flat that I am currently occupying. He kept complaining about the noise from the giant air conditioner that was opposite the kitchen window and about other things, as well. Mrs. Baillache told me that he was asked to leave. The individuals who had set out to help him felt frustrated, puzzled, and unappreciated as the situation worsened. I spoke to one of them, and he seemed to be a nice guy. "Call me Donald," he said. "You know, like Donald Duck!"

My flat, by the way, is not air-conditioned; only the offices in the building are. The noise from the building air conditioner is constant but I tune it out. It is like having a room air conditioner in your house running all the time—no big deal. There is a door midway down the outer hall that is adjacent to my apartment. When the hall door is closed, even more noise is shut out.

Donald came and put a slide bolt on the inside of my balcony door. It was only secured by a skeleton key and opened up into the main thoroughfare of the building. The front door has a deadbolt and chain. However, there are no cage doors with padlocks. I tell friends here that you can become a prisoner behind your security. I want to take reasonable precautions to keep intruders out, but I also want to be able to get out myself—quickly—in case of an emergency. A steel cage door and padlock slow you down. Plus, who wants to be locked inside with an intruder?

The flat is noisy during the day when the students are around; in the evening and on weekends, it is quiet. I do not want to live in a monastery. It is good to hear what is going on around you. Sometimes, though, I want human life to fade out so I can hear birds, monkeys, or even the wind, as well.

There are security guards that sometimes sit a short distance from my front door, usually on weekends. During the week, they are at the guard station, which I can see from my balcony window. All of the guards are black. Sometimes they have one of the German shepherds with them, Smokey or Rea. Cyprian is one of the guards. Whenever I see him, I bring scraps for the dog. Today I cut up some fresh cheddar cheese. Cyprian showed me how Rea would jump for it, and I told him to have some of the cheese himself, too. Smokey and Rea let me pet them. They do not bark when I approach. Cyprian says, "They know who is dangerous." The white South Africans in my office cannot believe the dogs would let me come near them, or that the guards would let me come near their dogs.

South Africa has come so far since the dismantling of apartheid six years ago, but prejudice and hostility are still very deep. Some white South Africans do not see the black workers as persons. They only see "black people." I get to know them by name. Clementine cleans the office. The other day she was on a balcony atop the physics building. I was walking to work and did not see her. I heard this sound like a giant winged insect from the rainforest—tizz, tizz, tizz. I looked around, then up, and Clementine was waving, "Hi, Doris!" Kay and Sagie are maintenance men in the Department of Biology. I call them the "dynamic duo." Patricia is a Zulu who delivers the mail. Ruth is a guard at the gate where I come and go when I leave the university grounds. Today she told me she had been up until 2 a.m. celebrating. Her granddaughter was entering Law School at UND. I congratulated her and told her how wonderful that was. Lorraine works at a shop I stop by once in a while; she claps her hands and giggles when she sees me. Royal is a laundromat attendant. She does the laundry for people who drop off their clothes. I do my laundry and talk to Royal. Whenever she sees me, she smiles and says, "Hello, my friend." I tell her what is going to happen on *Days of Our Lives*. The South African broadcasts are a year or more behind the US. So, I am Royal's crystal ball, and she loves it.

I try to respect, enjoy, and encourage all of the persons I meet—black, white, or any color. Of course, you cannot help but feel the stress from the increasing violence here. A week ago, Paul Denig, the Director of the United States Information Services, invited all the current Fulbrighters in the area for dinner at his home, which amounted to about six guests. He told us to be very aware and very careful. If we were someplace where shooting starts, we should keep our heads down and pray. That is one way to end a party and get the guests to leave early!

Squatter Camps

Right on the edge of the campus, squatter camps are growing daily. These arise as people come into the city because they have no jobs and no homes. The government is afraid to disperse the people because they do not want to be compared to the old apartheid government. The squatters piece together cardboard, cloth, and tin—whatever they can scrounge or steal. It is disturbing to see, and rightfully so. I know it would be dangerous to go into the camps alone. However, I want to see if my parish is doing any volunteer work there in groups. Perhaps, they bring clothes and food or teach the children.

My parish, by the way, is called Assumption. It is about a five-minute drive from my flat. I usually go to the 5:30 p.m. Mass on Saturday. The pastor (and sole priest) introduced himself to me, Derrick Butt. He is an Oblate of Mary Immaculate (OMI). The parish is largely white. There are black children in the parish school and a couple of black nuns. I met another priest from Blessed Sacrament Parish in North Durban, Fr. Carrington. He is past 80, but a lively guy. Fr. Carrington said that his order was originally the main one in Southern Africa. For Easter, I might go to his little church, Star of the Sea, at Umhlanga Beach.

The services at both Assumption and Blessed Sacrament seem a bit formal compared to parishes in the US, but they do have altar girls. When I talk to Fr. Butt about the squatter camps, I will learn to what extent the parish is involved in social justice efforts. It would be unfair to make a judgment based on the "whiteness" of the congregation. I do not know what is going on there. It would seem that the camps are within the parish boundaries or close, so maybe some of the organizations, like St. Vincent de Paul, are active there.

Many white South Africans are still fearful of black South

Africans. They think they all have HIV or AIDS. That is one reason they give for not intervening if they see someone being victimized. Plus, they do not want to get shot. There are other white South Africans, though, who are doing all they can to change things. The history of race in the US is just as scarred and complicated.

When Donald put the bolt on my door, a fellow named George popped in for a minute. After he left, Donald told me about George. He was a construction engineer for twenty years. Now he teaches at the university. On weekends, with building materials bought with his own money, he drives several hours north to Maputaland, which is known for its beautiful beaches. There, he helps the black South Africans construct homes and other buildings. According to Donald, it is the women who do most of the work. The men simply unload the supplies. "Down here," Donald said, "the women work hard." If you pay attention, you can see that. Overall, it is amazing that, even though the end of apartheid scarcely changed black lives economically, they still press on, still laugh, and still make plans for their children and grandchildren. When Martin Luther King Jr. spoke about the mountaintop, he said: "I may not get there with you, but . . . we as a people will get to the Promised Land."[17] Black South Africans endure and hope. I suppose that most people focus on the immediate demands and joys of their lives. That is why some politicians get away with so much and so little.

Rental Car

A lot of the violence here starts with carjacking and car theft. In some cases, the thieves shoot right through the car windows to get the car. People fortify their cars the way they fortify their homes—with lock-and-key bars for the steering wheel and the transmission stick, immobilizers for the ignition, and alarms for the doors.

---

[17] On 3 April 1968, Martin Luther King Jr. spoke in Memphis, Tennessee. The next day he was assassinated.

Cars are very expensive, even rental cars. I finally had to rent a car from the local "rent-a-wreck." They did fix some things on the car after I drove it the first weekend. For example, one door would not open and the fan would not work. Other things they just wrote off. The back window wiper does not work; in heavy rain, it is hard to see behind me. Fortunately, the probability of getting heavy rain very often is not high.

All in all, though, I am very satisfied with my little car. It is a 1989 VW Golf GSX, medium blue, four doors, hatchback, no radio, no air conditioning, and no passenger-side mirror. Still, it has a solid feel on the road, the body is in good shape, and it climbs hills easily. What more could you want? I have to pay about $555 US a month and get 1500 free km. After that, I pay about .70 Rand per km. The rental agency gave me a "gorilla bar" for the steering wheel, but then said they are virtually useless since the thieves just cut through the steering wheel. If the car is stolen or damaged, I have to pay a $420 US deductible. Gas here is expensive. Since the VW gets good gas mileage, I can drive quite a few km and still pay about $20 US a week in gas.

Yesterday (March 23), I was in the grocery store. As soon as the black check-out clerk heard my American accent, she asked how I liked South Africa. I said, "Fine but I just hope my car won't be stolen before I leave!" She laughed and said, "It won't because I'll be praying for you!" I am going to depend on those prayers more than I depend on the gorilla bar! That little story, I think, illustrates the sweetness of the people here. If they finally manage to make South Africa a real "rainbow nation," it will be paradise.[18]

---

[18] Archbishop Desmond Tutu spoke about South Africa as a "rainbow nation" with people of many colors and great potential. "You are the rainbow people of God," he said. In 1994 he published a book: *The Rainbow People of God*. His words recalled a passage from scripture: "I have set my rainbow in the clouds, and it will be the sign of the covenant between me and the earth." Genesis 9:13 NIV

Exchange Rates and Credit Cards

My Fulbright Award is a fixed amount. I will receive three more payments before the end of the year. These are deposited directly into a checking account in St. Louis. Everything that I can put on my MasterCard, I do. Then I call toll-free on the 19th of every month, and MasterCard tells me the amount of my bill. I write a check against my bank account in the US and airmail it to MasterCard.

When I came here in February, the exchange rate was 3.6 Rand to 1$ US. That has gone up to almost 3.9 Rand per 1$ US. The problem is that tomorrow it could go down to 1 Rand per 1$ US—or lower. All of that is unpredictable. The Rand crept up a little because people thought Nelson Mandela was ill and the future of the country, therefore, was uncertain. Then, it leveled off because Mandela went into the hospital, had all kinds of tests run, and walked out with a clean bill of health.

What does all this mean? Well, for example, my rent at the flat is 896 Rand per month, which is approximately $250 US. If next week the Rand went on parity with the US dollar, my rent would be $896 US. That is one of the bad things about living overseas. It is a financial gamble. Understandably, the Fulbright Program makes no adjustments for inflation or devaluation of the currency. You are on your own!

My Office

My office is on the top floor, three, in the biology building. This is a new building, constructed about ten years ago. When you get off the elevator, there is a list of faculty names. Mine is there—Dr. D. Schoenhoff—which seems strange. The building and offices are air-conditioned. This was a blessing in February. The entire month was scorching hot. From now until December, the weather should be fairly nice.

The office is very large. It has a big metal desk, a built-in glass bookcase (with one book!), a two-shelf storage cabinet, and a built-in table with a drawer on which my computer sits. One entire wall is windows. I see the blue sky above, the physics building across the way, and look down on a park-like setting below (the open area between the physics and biology buildings). Surprisingly, I am always being told how neat and clean I am. Working with botanists, I have turned over a new leaf! Even my flat has been declared to be neat and clean. "I wish everyone who lived here," says Mrs. Baillache, "were as neat and clean." Some of the genes that Roland and Mary Ann inherited must have also been lying dormant in my body as well. Or, maybe this is just Kloof's Cleaning Syndrome, a disease I got from drinking the water (just kidding). By the way, I do drink the water right from the tap. No bottled water for me! Supposedly, the water is safe here, and I have not been sick at all in my first seven weeks.

My Job

This Thursday, March 28, I will be giving a seminar on *The Barefoot Expert* to honors students and biology faculty. Part of my talk will be about expert systems and fuzzy logic. Also, I will be undertaking a project that Pat Berjak is very excited about. This will entail designing a multimedia database for IPUP (Indigenous Plant Usage Project). At the start, I will be driving about 180 km north of Durban to begin gathering information on local plants and trees. My mentors will be a fellow named Ian Gardiner[19] and his Zulu worker, Jobe Mafuleka.

---

[19] Ian Garland was a well-known and well-respected conservationist in South Africa. He has been described as a reluctant sugarcane farmer who turned his life's work into saving the environment and planting trees. In 1952, he established the Twin Streams Environmental Education Centre, the first of its kind in South Africa. The center was named for his farm, Twin Streams. The two streams cutting across his land are the Amanzimnyama and the Siyaya rivers. To care for the environment, Ian encouraged people to make a difference, including planting trees and being aware of the importance of water to life on our planet. He estimated that he had planted 60,000 trees in his lifetime. Ian died in 2007 at the age of 82.

I was told that Ian is the father of indigenous plant study in Natal. Ian calls Jobe a "fundi." That is a natural expert in local botanical knowledge. Jobe knows what the Zulu call the plants and how they use them for medicinal purposes. The relationship between the two men is very interesting. Jobe speaks no English, but Ian speaks Zulu. Their mutual trust and respect are visible. I also sense their common awareness that they are both old and their knowledge may be lost. More than that, something that they love may be lost. No one has ever asked to capture the knowledge these two men have. With Pat's encouragement, I will make a start.

Ian is in Australia for a month, visiting family. When he returns, I will go up to his "heritage site" to begin some filming with his son-in-law, Gavin Hough. This film will later be incorporated into a multimedia database. Gavin is a physicist, and we get on well. He will be providing some of the technology to scan the plant specimens and create a digital image. Even three-dimensional objects, like branches, can be scanned. We are going to look into using some NASA technology to help analyze specimens and learn more about the environment the plant was in and the stress it was under. Yes, plants get stressed too! It is all very exciting and challenging. Pat has also asked me to give a post-graduate seminar on the Internet and possibly give some other public talks outside the university. Presently, I do not know if there will be time for that. The project with Ian will keep me very busy.

Television

In the seven weeks I have been in South Africa, I have only had a TV for five days. Mrs. Baillache lent me her small, color TV. While I was watching it, I heard a whizzing sound. Then the picture went blank, the sound stopped, and smoke came out of the back of the TV. It is in for repairs. If they can fix it cheaply enough, I will rent it from Mrs. Baillache for forty Rand a month. I would like to have it for CNN and some of the good programs. There are only three channels and two of the channels often carry programs in one of the eleven local African languages. As a result, there is only one channel to watch, unless you pay for a very expensive satellite hookup.

Mary Ann was surprised to learn we get the American soap operas here, like *Days of Our Lives*, *Santa Barbara*, and *The Young and the Restless*. I kiddingly told her to send me the plots so I can sell the information to all the addicts of the "soapies." When I give them the scoop on what is going to happen next, they can amaze their friends with their clairvoyance. Recently at the laundromat, I told Royal that John Black becomes a priest, Marlena is possessed by the devil and has an exorcism, and Sammy has a baby by Austin. Her mouth was wide open, and then she said, "Ooh, I can't wait to tell my friend!" Of course, I told Mary Ann we are missing out on a business opportunity. We could be the "Psychics to the Soaps." Nah, I was only kidding!

We also get other American programs, like *Oprah* (twice a day), and *The Commish*, about a police commissioner in a small suburb of New York. There is a definite upside to being without TV, namely, I am reading a lot. Right now, I am reading a book on quantum physics and complexity, *The Quark and the Jaguar*, another on fuzzy logic, and a third called *Being Digital* by the head of the MIT Media Lab. When I have time, I fit in a few murder mysteries too.

Paperback books are expensive. Ordinary novels are around $10 to $15 US. Technical books and textbooks are very expensive. As a result, a lot of books are stolen from the libraries. In the computer field, the university library is practically useless, because the books and journals are not up-to-date. I depend on the Internet, not just to get my CNN news every day but to find information on artificial intelligence and expert systems. Sometimes service bogs down as more and more people start using it. The library does have a fantastic view of the Durban skyline, though, with the Indian Ocean in the background. Once in a while, I go there just to see the view.

Shopping Malls

Yes, South Africa has them. I can see the biggest one in Durban, the Pavilion, in the distance from my balcony. Architecturally, it is a cross between the Kremlin and a maharaja's palace.

The malls here are like American malls with a couple of large stores, a lot of eating places, some cinemas, and little specialty shops. The big difference is that the large department stores do not have anywhere near the selection we do. There might be two brands of bedsheets in six colors. A lot of the specialty stores are geared toward tourists and local crafts. Plus, the malls do not stay open as late as ours. There is too much worry about crime, and people are reluctant to go out at night.

Everything tends to go into the shopping mall, including the grocery stores. You cannot just drive up to a Schnucks or a Dierbergs. You have to go to Musgrave Center, the Pavilion, or La Lucia Mall.

Cinemas

I have only been to one cinema in Durban, and that was to see *To Die For*, starring Nicole Kidman. When you buy a ticket, they print your seat number on it. You cannot simply sit wherever you want. I found this out because I was sitting in some man's seat and he politely asked me to move. The movie seat, by the way, was like a plush recliner chair, and just as hard to get out of. The movies are fairly recent. Right now, *Jumanji*, *Sense and Sensibility*, *Heat*, and *Casino* are playing, along with others.

Durban

Durban is right on the Indian Ocean. There are nice beaches both north and south of the city. I do not enjoy going into the city because of the traffic congestion. Some of the drivers are reckless. Getting a parking place is only slightly easier than winning the lottery. The streets are somewhat dangerous even during the day. The girlfriend of one of the Fulbrighters was mugged in broad daylight only three weeks after she arrived here. No one intervened on her behalf. They just walked on by. When Paul Denig and his wife stayed in the five-star Royal Hotel, they saw a man killed from their hotel window. I told them that I stayed at that hotel when I came to Durban on business for McDonnell Douglas, and a camera was stolen from my room.

The trees that line the streets in the suburbs are beautiful, with flowers of purple and white, yellow and pink. Some have a wonderful fragrance that takes you by surprise as you walk by. The old homes are probably lovely too, but it is difficult to see them behind the brick walls and the security gates.

About three hours north of Durban is Hluhluwe, one of the main game parks in South Africa. I had been there before when I came to South Africa on business. However, I wanted to go back, so I went on a tour. There were only four of us in a minibus. The tour cost 450 Rand, about $125 US. It was wonderful. We saw lots of animals, like giraffes, rhinos, and impala.

Coincidentally, when Pat Berjak heard that I was going to Hluhluwe, she asked if I would bring back some fruit from the marula trees for their seed program. The fruit is about the size of a large nectarine. When it ripens and falls off the trees, all kinds of animals eat it, including elephants, baboons, giraffes, ostrich, and wart hogs. Elephants are not patient enough to let the fruit fall; they simply shake the trees. When the fruit is fermented in the stomachs of the elephants, they get drunk and stagger around. The headline in the paper about three weeks ago was "Drunken Giraffe Kills Man." I should have saved it.

Anyway, we did come across some marula trees in the park. I asked the driver if I could get out and collect some of their fruit. I had brought white plastic bags with me. The driver was reluctant because there were animals in the area. None of the passengers were interested in fruit picking either, not that I blamed them! Before I left the minibus, I spoke to the driver. "If I don't come back, I can see the headline," I said. "American Marula-Poacher Killed by Lion—News at Eleven!" At two different spots, the driver stopped and I gathered the marula fruit. Inside the minibus, my marula haul smelled like fermenting wine. Of course, it had to go under my seat all the way home. When I told Pat Berjak that I risked my life for science, she quickly said, "You're an absolute star." For sure, the students who had to crack that marula fruit to get the seeds did not think so. If you are not an elephant, it is pretty tough!

Sani Pass and Lesotho

On March 31, I took a tour of the Drakensberg, the "Mountains of the Dragon." Great name, huh! Some of the peaks in the Drakensberg are among the highest on the African continent. I booked the trip through Shaka Tours, named after the Zulu king and warrior. There was only one other person on the tour. It was a woman from Brazil, who was about eighty years old. Her name was Renata. The tour guide's name was Rob. We drove in a white Toyota minivan. I sat in the front seat because Renata did not like to wear a seat belt; it bothered her neck and gave her a headache. Rob picked me up at about 7:15 a.m. on a Sunday, right by one of the security gates at the University of Natal.

About an hour down the road, Renata asked Rob to detour to Pietermaritzburg, because she had not had a chance to see it on her South African tour. This was not on our tour, and I said I was not keen to go there. I booked for the mountains, not the city. Understandably, Rob complied with Renata's request. As the day progressed, though, there were more requests. Renata had been used to private tours up to that point, and she wanted to stop where and when she chose. Also, she drove Rob crazy with questions. "Can we stop here and look inside the native huts?" Renata asked. "No, dear, and please try to say ethnic, not native," Rob said "When the natives wave at us, what are they thinking?" Renata asked. "Do they like us?" Rob replied, "I have no idea, dear." At one point we passed a long line of Zulus marching down the road with their traditional sticks raised in the air like spears. Rob was a little nervous because he did not know if it was a protest. Renata asked, "Can we stop and take a picture of them?" Rob replied, "No, dear!" Then he speeded up.

In addition to all these questions, Renata kept telling Rob how she had to stop every few hours for food or there would be dire consequences. She had a medical condition. We never learned what the medical condition was. We stopped for lunch at a very nice hotel. Lunch was served outside and we had a good view of part of the mountain range. The clouds were hanging low, so we could not see the peaks.

As we drove through the mountains, we saw some beautiful scenery. In some cases, there were whole fields of pink flowers called Cosmos. Once we drove near a river, and I wished I had been prepared to snap a picture. In seconds, we were down the road, and the picture was gone. In my mind, though, I can still see the African women washing their clothes in the river. On an outcrop of rock were some naked children sunning themselves on their bellies, like babies on a bearskin rug! Their wet bodies glistened in the light. They giggled and clapped as we drove by.

Our only stop on the afternoon drive (other than a shopping stop for Renata) was Howick Falls. Renata did not want to get out of the car since she said she had Iguazu Falls near her in Latin America. That is one of the most beautiful falls in the entire world. Remember the movie *The Mission*, where the Jesuit goes over the falls on a cross? That was Iguazu Falls. Anyway, I slid out of the van, and, reluctantly, so did Renata. It turned out that Howick Falls was beautiful too. It is created by the sheer plunge of the Mgeni River (or Umgeni in Zulu) into a very lush, green area. The falls are about 300 feet high. I lingered quite a while near the railing, just taking it all in.

When we left the falls, it began to rain. Within an hour, it was raining quite hard. By the time we reached Robin's Nest, our bed and breakfast stop for the first leg of the journey, Rob was not speaking to Renata; more accurately, he was ignoring her. At one point when we were alone, he referred to her as Dr. Ruth, presumably because she was always speculating about what the "natives" thought and felt.[20] "Why isn't Rob talking to me?" she asked. "What have I done?" I just laughed and suggested we enjoy the day.

At Robin's Nest, Renata and I were supposed to share a room. Double occupancy would have saved each of us 400 Rand—about $100 US. When the hotel owner showed us our room with two beds, Renata asked her, "Where do I sleep?" I suggested that Renata choose either bed. Renata told the owner that I was a "dear person" with a wonderful sense of humor, but she could not sleep in the same room with another human being—not even her sister. She said she had a medical condition that made this impossible. So, yippee, I got a room to myself with a lovely garden view, and Rob did not insist that I pay the additional 400 Rand.

We had dinner at about 8:00 p.m. This is typical for South Africans, but late for me. It was a good steak dinner. Renata did not want steak because she was worried about the cows in England that were infected with mad cow disease. She thought some of the meat might have found its way to South Africa. I ate the steak. It was like the sign on my kitchen wall in St. Louis: "You have two choices for dinner— take it or leave it." There were no menus. The meal was very good. However, I have virtually stopped eating meat since I came to South Africa. Normally, I just eat fish. We will see how long that lasts! Since Durban is on the coast, the fish are fresh. Often, I will pop fish with curry sauce or fish with mozzarella and feta cheese into the microwave, and beep-beep dinner is served. Hopefully, I will not find out on CNN that there is mad halibut disease!

In the morning, I played a bit with the two German shepherds at

---

[20] Karola Ruth Westheimer (Dr. Ruth) is an outspoken sex therapist, author, and talk show guest in the US. She was born in Germany and her Jewish parents died in the Holocaust.

the house. One was called Shaka and the other Misha. Misha would take the cuff of my jeans in her mouth and lift my leg about three feet off the ground. Then she would grab my wrist with her teeth and drag me around. She was still a puppy, only seven months old. She wanted to play!

The truck that was going to take us to the top of Sani Pass came about 10 a.m., an hour late. It was a Toyota pickup truck with four-wheel drive. The driver's name was Jonathan. Two ladies were already in the truck. They were going to the top of Sani Pass to do some hiking. The one in the front seat was in her seventies and the one in the back was in her fifties. I ended up sandwiched in the middle of the back seat between Bridgette and Renata.

We drove to the border of South Africa and Lesotho. Lesotho is a tiny kingdom surrounded by South Africa. At that point, we had to present our passports. Afterward, I decided to jump into the back of the pickup truck so I would have a better view. Bridgette got in the back with me. One of the African workmen was already in the back of the truck. I made myself comfortable on a cement bag, and the Toyota started up Sani Pass. The road was rough; holes and large rocks were everywhere. It was hard going even with the four-wheel drive. The road went right along the edge of Sani Pass and up for about 10,000 feet. I saw beautiful views, actually a 360-degree perspective.

At the top of Sani Pass is a tiny lodge. It was very basic—maybe a rating of half a star. While the others went into the lodge, I walked further up the mountain. At one point, it started to rain, a very cold rain. So, I headed back to the lodge to dry out before the fire and have a good lunch.

After lunch, Jonathan took me and Renata to see the little general store. It was very clean on the inside and well organized with a few can goods, some clothes, a new camp bed, and other things. Some teenage Basotho boys were standing inside. I noticed four of them. They wore blankets. Underneath were their underpants or nothing. They are very poor. Jonathan took us inside one of the African huts so we could see how they live. Again, it was very well-swept and very clean. There was a mat on the floor for sleeping. However, there was no furniture and just a little open cabinet with a few dishes. A woman stood by the mat and drew back a blanket. There were two tiny babies sleeping side by side. They appeared to be twins and were all bundled up with knitted caps on their heads. One was a boy and one was a girl. I thought of Mary Ann and Roland! Jonathan asked the woman their names. She responded in Sesotho, so I do not know what the names were. Jonathan said one of the names meant "I hope I have more children."

The people there have very little. If any of you are ever at some good after-season sales at Kmart or Target, please pick up some clothes for infants, children, and teens. Include clothes for cold weather as well as warm. Even though this is Africa, it gets very cold in the mountains during the winter. Just send them by surface mail, because it is cheaper. It may take months for the package to get here, but when the clothes arrive, I will see that Jonathan takes them to the families atop Sani Pass. He works up there and goes up every day with his tour business. Just a suggestion! No way can I get clothes as cheap here in South Africa as in the States, or get as much variety and quality.

Mr. Toad's Wild Ride

When Jonathan was ready to head down the mountain, I told him I wanted to ride in the back again. Renata and I were the only two going back. She rode in the front seat of the truck with Jonathan. I climbed into the back of the truck. Only this time, the bed of the truck was covered with large, metal containers that I thought were milk containers—the kind you see on dairy farms. Jonathan told me to just sit on top of the containers, which I did. As we started down the mountain, I looked at the container under my butt and it said "GAS." I just hoped that all the containers were empty and going back for a refill!

As soon as we started the descent, I realized I had made a mistake, but there was no turning back. Jonathan was driving faster than he should have since he was an hour late. The road had hairpin turns; they call one section the Zig Zags. The road was right on the edge of the mountain and, of course, there were no guard rails. This is the outback of Africa! Well, I thought as big as I am that I would be as stable as a rock on those containers. Wrong! The containers and I were bouncing right out of the bed of the truck like ping pong balls in a lottery barrel. Since I was sitting on top of rolling cylinders, my center of gravity was way above the bed of the truck. I figured the physics out pretty quickly. So did my rear end. At one point, I was thrown onto my back. I had no place to grip the rolling cylinders, and the truck kept bouncing and shooting downward. I thought for sure I was going to roll right off the top and into the canyon below. Without turning around, I tried slamming my fist on the back window of the truck and shouting, but no one responded. It was April Fools' Day. Of course, I said to myself, "More the fool you for getting into this mess!" I was scared to death. I do not know what kept me in that truck. However, I did get spectacular views of Sani Pass. Maybe sometimes you have to take a risk for beauty and knowledge. Had I known the risk I was taking, I do not think I would have done it, but maybe I would have.

When we reached the Lesotho border, Jonathan stopped. I was beginning to think he forgot where the brake pedal was. I stood up and then almost fell out of the back of the truck from dizziness. Jonathan caught my hand. I said, "Jonathan, if anyone ever asks you if they can ride down Sani Pass in the back of your pickup truck, say no, it's too dangerous!" Then I told him what had been going on. He had no idea I was in trouble. Of course, I could not help but be excited and laugh too. I told him, "That was better than Mr. Toad's Wild Ride!" After I explained to him who Mr. Toad was and about the ride at Disney World, he was excited. I think next time he will sell tickets for the ride in the back of his truck!

At the border control, I reached for my passport in my shirt pocket. It was not there. I thought, "What next?" Jonathan looked in the bed of the truck and found my passport under some of the metal gas cylinders. It had flown out of my pocket when I got thrown on my back. At the passport window, Renata turned to me and said, "Oh, Doris, good thing you couldn't see where we were going because it was very scary." This was from a woman who was sitting in the front seat of the truck with a seatbelt on and the window up! She thought I had missed the show. On the contrary, I was the show! I am just glad I have an exciting tale to tell, instead of a white cross on the slopes of Sani Pass.

After that, going home was anti-climactic. We ran into a lot of rain and a highway accident that forced us to detour for about an hour. Renata broke out her crackers and reminded us she needed food. No crackers were passed to the front seat. When he could, Rob stopped at a little convenience store to let Renata run in and buy something to eat. He got out of the car to light a cigarette. "No, that's okay, I won't go in," Renata said from the back seat. "I don't want to hold you up." I just said, "Let's go, Renata." Then, we left Rob muttering by the van. Once inside the store, Renata could not decide what she wanted. I picked up a Tinkie which is the same as our Twinkie and extolled its virtues: nice sponge cake; cream center; something light that will not bother your stomach this late at night. Renata bought it, crawled in the backseat of the van, and said, "You know just what my stomach needs, Doris."

While I was often surprised during the trip by Renata's questions and requests, I admire the fact that she still travels alone at eighty years old. She was just used to being spoiled, as she said, and wanted some attention and service. Renata phoned me before she left Durban and said she was going to call me from Johannesburg before she left for South Africa and write to me from Brazil. Who does not enjoy getting a letter from a well-traveled friend?

KwaZulu Natal

Just an ounce of history! Durban, where I live, is in the KwaZulu Natal province of South Africa. Before Nelson Mandela became the first black president of South Africa, this province was simply called Natal. After Mandela became president, a couple of the provinces were redrawn and renamed—Africanized! Natal became KwaZulu Natal. The province that contains Johannesburg, the largest South African city, was renamed Gauteng. If you happen to read (as I did before I left St. Louis) that KwaZulu Natal is "ground zero" for violence in South Africa, it is largely between members of the IFP (Inkatha Freedom Party) and the ANC (African National Congress). Mandela, head of the ANC, is a Xhosa. Chief Mangosuthu Buthelezi, head of the IFP, is a Zulu. The Xhosas and the Zulus are longtime rivals.

As the name suggests, KwaZulu Natal is the old stomping grounds of Shaka and his half-brother, Dingane, the great Zulu leaders. There was a good mini-series on TV a few years ago called "Shaka Zulu." If I had a VCR, I would rent the movie and watch it. You could do that in St. Louis. I did buy a Zulu language tape to see if I can pick up at least a few phrases in the language.

Of course, a lot of the violence in South Africa comes not from tribal differences but from homelessness, joblessness, anger, and bitterness. It is directed against whites, primarily through home break-ins, carjacking, and rape. Some of these crimes, as you would expect, end in murder, too.

On Monday, April 15, the Truth and Reconciliation Commission, headed by Archbishop Desmond Tutu, began hearing from ordinary people who had stories of suffering, torture, and murder under apartheid. When the new constitution was formed, anyone who committed crimes to further the political aim of apartheid ("apartness" based on race) was granted amnesty under the law. Supposedly, this was to prevent a bloodbath when black Africans were given political power. Yet, a lot of black Africans are angry. They want justice and compensation.

Some of the Commission hearings will be televised. I hope to watch them, difficult though that may be. It will be an education in itself.[21]

The other morning on TV there was something about Steven Spielberg and the Shoah Project.[22] In World War 11, six million Jews throughout German occupied territory were murdered in what is called Shoah or the Holocaust (1941-1945). The Shoah Project will preserve the witness and stories of as many survivors as possible. Each time you hear one of the stories, it tears your heart out. One recalled prisoners praying as they went to the gas chambers: "God, where are you now?" The program mentioned the powerful witness of Elie Wiesel, an author and survivor of the Holocaust.[23]

Living in another country is a good time to learn its history. So often, with little necessity, Americans know little about our own history. If we do not know where we came from, we cannot deeply know ourselves. I have been reading a book by James Gregory called *Goodbye Bafana*. Gregory was Mandela's prison warden for 20 of the 27 years that Mandela was in prison. In addition, I am reading Mandela's *Long Walk to Freedom*. When I am finished, I promised to give the book to Royal, the attendant at the laundromat where I go each week. She is the one who is always asking about the "soapies." Also, she tells me how much she "loves" Princess Diana and "hates" Prince Charles.

---

[21] Desmond Tutu was a husband, father of four children, Anglican priest, archbishop, theologian, and author. He was also a leader in the protests against apartheid in South Africa. Four times he was nominated for the Nobel Peace Prize, winning it finally in 1984. His voice carried beyond South Africa as well. He spoke out against the Vietnam War, the fighting between Israelis and Palestinians, and the strife in Northern Ireland. He died at the age of 90 on 26 December 2021. As tributes poured in, one nun recalled his hot pink robes and said he "beamed love."

[22] The Shoah Project began in 1994, interestingly the same year as the end of apartheid in South Africa. In 2006, the permanent home of the institute was relocated to the University of Southern California. There are at least 55,000 audio-visual testimonies from holocaust survivors.

[23] In 1944, Elie Wiesel was sent to Auschwitz with his family. He was fifteen years old. His mother and sister were immediately murdered. Elie and his father were transferred to Buchenwald where his father died. Wiesel wrote extensively about the Holocaust, including his trilogy, *Night, Dawn,* and *Day*. In 1986 Wiesel won the Nobel Peace Prize. He died 2 July 2016.

It amazes me that she would have any feelings at all for Diana and Charles, much less such strong ones. She said it is because Diana is "so beautiful." Maybe the Royal Family is just like another "soapie" for her and perhaps for some Brits too.

Getting Around

It is an interesting time to be in South Africa, but a bit dangerous and stressful too. I try to enjoy my time here without taking stupid chances. That means that, generally, I do not go out in the evening. I have made a couple of exceptions, like a dinner party at Paul Denig's home in North Durban. His neighborhood is upscale. I have also been to dinner in the evening at the Pavilion and Musgrave Center, two large shopping centers with parking. For the most part, though, I stay home in the evenings, reading or watching TV. During the day, though, I go anywhere, as this Easter itinerary will show.

Easter Week—Holy Thursday

The Easter holiday began on Holy Thursday. I was on my way someplace (Fulham's bakery!) in the afternoon, when I saw a very large, old, white St. Bernard wandering around without a collar. She was ambling in and out of the traffic. I did a U-turn and stopped my car in the area she was walking. Then I went up to her and petted her, but I did not know what to do with her. So, I got back in my car and just watched her. Back again she went into the traffic and crossed Francois, the main street that runs by the University of Natal. This time, I drove my car across Francois and pulled into a driveway. As I was getting out of the car, a black man was throwing rocks at the dog. Maybe he was scared. The dog was not approaching him, and she did not even bark when he threw the rocks. She just tried to feint and duck. When the man saw me hurrying over, he moved on.

I tried to coax the dog into my little VW by opening the back door. The dog looked in the door as if to say, "You think I'm going to fit in there?" Then the dog looked at me. I looked at the dog. Finally, I looked at the houses. The houses are so fortified with high fences and electronic gates that I did not even know how to find a doorbell to ring. Plus, I did not want to leave the dog. In short, I did not know what to do.

Eventually, I got in my car, sped back to my apartment (about three minutes away), and phoned the SPCA, which happens to be practically in the university's backyard. A woman answered, and I told her about the dog. The woman began to give me a lecture about how 50,000 dogs are put down each year in Durban and how all pets should be on leashes. "Hey, I'm not the dog owner," I said. "I'm the dog rescuer." Also, I told her that I would pay to advertise for its owner because the dog was well-fed and someone's pet. The person I spoke to took the directions (near the intersection of Francois and Manning) and said she would send someone out to find the dog. Meanwhile, I worried.

Earlier in the week, Cyprian had told me that Smokey, the German shepherd I had played with and given treats to, had died. The cause was a snake bite. Cyprian said the people at the kennel had left the dog lying paralyzed and in agony from noon until 8 p.m. Finally, a vet came and gave the dog a lethal injection. Once before, Cyprian told me the guard dogs are ill-fed and mistreated. When one of the female German shepherds was pregnant, it was tied to a post. Guards kicked the dog repeatedly in the belly until its puppies aborted. Cyprian was heartsick about Smokey, and after I heard the story, so was I. The last thing I wanted was another unhappy ending for the stray St. Bernard.

At 7:30 in the evening, I went to my parish church, Assumption, for Holy Thursday. I arrived there shortly before Mass was scheduled to start. Perhaps that is why I ended up in the first pew on the right-hand side. The only other person seated beside me was a little African boy named Peter. I learned his name because I talked to him while we were waiting. At the liturgy, half of the prayers and hymns were in Zulu and half were in English. The priest consecrated the bread in Zulu and the wine in English. That evening I stayed in the church until midnight. The church was open for prayer before the Blessed Sacrament. I have to admit that I snuck in a prayer for the wandering St. Bernard! As I left the church, I was not afraid to go home in the dark. About a dozen people were walking out to their cars. The evening was beautiful. Before getting in my car, I stopped to look at the Southern Cross in the night sky. That is one of my favorite constellations, and I had not seen it since I left New Zealand. There it is even brighter. On the New Zealand flag is an image of the Southern Cross.

Good Friday

Good Friday morning I was driving down Francois and took a left on Manning. Right away I saw this man walking a large white St. Bernard with only a rope tied around her neck. Again, I stopped my car, went up to the man, and asked, "Is this your dog?" He said it was. I then told him what had happened the previous day. He thanked me again and again. He said the SPCA had come, and a neighbor saw the truck. She hollered out that she knew the dog and came down. When the SPCA reached the dog, it was standing in front of a tall gate. This is right where I left it, not knowing the dog just wanted me to open the gate so it could go home.

The dog's owner said his name was Dennis and the dog's name was Sally. Dennis said they were both a "landmark" in the area because he always walked Sally the same route every day. Everybody knew her since she was so big and so white. Sure enough, the route he was taking her was the same one Sally took on her own the day before. Sally, he said, was one of the family and they would have been heartbroken if she had been hit by a car. According to Dennis, Sally had never gotten out by herself before but, at that time, the family had a student-renter moving out of their home. The student left the gate open when she was taking her suitcases to the car. Exit Sally! Well, at least this tale had a happy ending.

It was nice to talk to Dennis, as well. He mentioned the recent plane crash in Croatia that killed Ron Brown, the US Secretary of Commerce, and 32 other Americans when their plane plowed into a mountain. Dennis had never flown. He said, "Can you imagine a man my age that has never been on an airplane?" I recalled that the TV news only gave information about the "important" people on the plane, like Brown and the corporate CEOs. Dennis said very simply, "I think each of us is important." It is funny how you get into these touching discussions with strangers. Or is it just me? Of course not!

That afternoon I happened to meet up with Cyprian again. He was on guard duty in the underground garage that is adjacent to my flat. He had Rea with him, a beautiful German shepherd. I went to my flat and brought out dog biscuits for Rea as well as a Coca-Cola and chocolate chip muffin for Cyprian. Cyprian was surprised how Rea would sit for me and jump. Everybody around the university seems to be afraid of the guard dogs. Cyprian said, "She'll never forget you." We talked. We talked about Smokey. We talked about God. We talked about books. Cyprian likes to read. I told him I would give him James Gregory's book, *Goodbye Bafana*. We talked some more. I took a few pictures of Cyprian and Rea so Cyprian will have them as a keepsake. I think he is afraid that Rea will get ill too or be mistreated, and that will be the last he sees of her. He wants to call the SPCA and tell them how the dogs are neglected. On the other hand, he is worried about his job if he does. During the conversation, Cyprian asked me why I did not stay in Africa. He said, "I like your style!" I laughed. It was a funny thing to say to someone like me, who has never been known for style. After a while, I told him I had to head to church. Cyprian said he would say his prayers as he sat in the empty garage. When I was about halfway across the garage and heading to my flat, Cyprian shouted out, "DORIS!" As I turned around, he made the sign of the cross, folded his hands, and bowed. I am not sure what he meant—probably that he was starting to say his prayers. I just smiled, waved, and walked on.

Shortly after that, I arrived at Assumption Church for Good Friday services at 3 p.m. Some of the young people of the parish put on a Passion play that was pretty good, except you could see some of them reading their lines off of spear points and Roman robes. A rather nerdy off-stage voice spoke all of Jesus' lines. Jesus looked like a jock with a great body, but I suspect maybe not a great memory!

Holy Saturday

On Holy Saturday, I went to Assumption for the evening service at 7:30 p.m. Again, it was half in Zulu and half in English. The priest wore this beautiful chasuble that was white with a large map of Africa on it. The map looked like the color of the African earth here—red-brown. On the southern tip of the map, were two white round African huts or rondavels. Above the map was a cross that looked like it was made of Zulu spears or at least was a Zulu design. The Mass was about two hours and thirty minutes long. In dismissing the congregation, the priest said, "Let's be thankful Christmas only comes once a year!" Christmas? The service was long, but not that long!

Easter Sunday

On Easter, I drove to Umhlanga Beach, about twenty minutes from my flat. I parked on a vacant lot and walked about two blocks to the Umhlanga Sands Hotel, right on the beach. I asked the rates at the desk—just out of curiosity. The desk clerk said it cost 650 Rand for two persons, one night. That is about $160 US. I said to myself, "I don't think I'll be checking in my bags." Instead, I got a table in the lounge area that faced the Indian Ocean. Then I ordered grilled shrimp, butternut squash, creamed spinach, and rice. That was my Easter dinner!

After lunch, I went out on a balcony and watched the sunbathers for a while. I arrived just in time to see the small children hunting around the pool area for Easter eggs. I know, that sounds more like Miami than Africa!

Easter Monday—April 8

On the Monday after Easter, I met up with Kathleen Bethel. She is a proud black woman from Chicago who has a six-month grant to work at a library in Durban. When we first met, Kathleen jokingly told me that in the "new" South Africa I am on the B-Team. I laughed, but point taken. We drove to a pottery show at the home of Andrew Walford, whom the local Sunday paper called the "foremost South African potter." Walford's home is in Showgeni, known for horse breeding. It is in a beautiful wooded area with a magnificent view of the nearby hills and the Showgeni Dam. For 15 Rand, about $3.75 US, I bought a small piece of pottery, two glasses of home-made lemonade, a hot-cross bun, and a seat on his back lawn with a million-dollar view. That would be hard to beat!

Afterward, Kathleen and I drove to the Rob Roy Hotel, overlooking Thousand Hills. This time it was a clear day and you really could see forever, or almost. When I went there for the first time, on March 21, there was morning fog and I could not even see one hill much less a thousand. We ate lunch out on the back lawn, where we could take in the view. I had a toasted tuna sandwich and a chocolate shake for lunch. The shake was nothing like those at Ted Drewes Frozen Custard or Dairy Queen. It was just chocolate milk that was "shaken, not stirred."

On the drive home, we stopped at a gift shop. Kathleen purchased about five items and ordered an African wrap skirt. I bought a very old Pende mask from Zaire. It was used in a ceremonial dance to cure madness. You can see how it will come in handy for me! The face is asymmetrical. In addition, one side of the face is black—the sane, happy side. The other side is white—the mad, sad side. It is now hanging on the wall of my flat. Every time I see it, I think, "I must've been mad to buy that." If not, I will go mad staring at it, while it stares back at me![24]

Easter Tuesday

On Tuesday I drove myself downtown to get my visa renewed. The powers that be will not issue a visa for the entire year. They want you to come back again and again, fill out the forms, and wait in the queues. It is a common form of bureaucratic torture, but I am tough and now I am legal again until October.

Easter Wednesday

On Wednesday, I went to see a matinee performance of *Agnes of God* at the downtown playhouse. The advertising was a bit over the top, as they say here. There were posters taped on downtown street corners that read "Nun Kills Baby in Attic." This was followed by the box office phone number for "further information." The actors did a great job though. When I came home, I wrote them a note telling them so. I do not think the audience appreciated the quality of the performance, not that I am in any way a drama critic. Some South Africans have told me that the arts were neglected under the old National Party government. The isolation that South Africa experienced at that time only made matters worse. Talented artists and actors simply stayed away.

---

[24] The mask still hangs on a wall in my home. At one point I sent photos to the St. Louis Art Museum and was told that it definitely appears genuine. However, I never took it to an appraiser of African art as suggested. For me, its value is in my memory.

Sunday—April 14

On Sunday I went to hear the Natal Philharmonic Orchestra perform in the botanical garden. The concert was not until 3 p.m., but I arrived at about 11 a.m. I found a great parking spot right near the entrance, spent the afternoon in the gardens, found a park bench right by the lake, and enjoyed the orchestra playing. It was wonderful. At the same time, I was watching dozens of beautiful White Egrets circle overhead and roost in the trees on the islets in the lake. One heron looked as though it was wading in light as the sun sparkled on the water. Two large turtles were swimming about. Over my head were the branches of a big tree that hung above the water. When the sun shone through the tree, it was like a shadow of fire on the leaves. Beautiful!

The orchestra played some classical selections, like the *William Tell Overture*. The Russian orchestra leader told the crowd that they would immediately recognize the song. I thought his hint was the theme from *The Lone Ranger*. Instead, he meant it was used in a toothpaste ad here. A different generation, a different culture! The orchestra also played a medley from *Phantom of the Opera* and *Fiddler on the Roof*. The latter is playing here now, and I will probably go to a matinee on Saturday. The horn section did some jazz tunes, like *Basin Street Blues*. The orchestra ended with John Philip Sousa's *Stars and Stripes Forever*. It was great. Imagine all that music for about $3.75 US! The week after Easter, the students were all on vacation, so that is why I did so much merrymaking in one week. Not that one should ever need an excuse for merrymaking!

Sibongile Khumalo—April 20

I had been running errands on Saturday. When I returned to the campus, I noticed a poster on a lamp post right near the security gate. It was advertising a concert at the Elizabeth Sneddon Theatre, the university's performing arts center. I had seen the poster before, but since I had never heard of the performer—Sibongile Khumalo—I did not pay much attention. On the spur of the moment, I decided to go to the first performance of the evening at 6 p.m.

I went to Sneddon at about 5:15 p.m. and, for $10 US, got a single ticket in the first row, one seat off dead center. Soon as I started to read through the program, I knew I was in for a treat. Printed in the program were well-wishes from Nelson Mandela and Yehudi Menuhin, among others. By the time the show started, the theater was full.

Sibongile Khumalo had a beautiful voice and sang traditional African music, as well as *Ave Maria* and *Amazing Grace*. She said she wants to "create music that is fulfilling, inspirational, and deeply spiritual in nature." This is a plus-size lady, and so were her three backup singers. That said, you could tell that they all thought of themselves as beautiful. No self-esteem problems here! Their African caftans were as bright and bold as the women themselves. I thoroughly enjoyed the show. On the way out of the theater, I bought a tape of Sibongile's first album, *Ancient Evenings*, for about $7.50 US.

That weekend Tina Turner was also in town. She was kicking off her world tour—*Golden Eye*—here in South Africa. Tickets for her show were 200 Rand, almost five times what Sibongile Khumalo's concert cost. There was a big TV advertising blitz leading up to the performance. Tina Turner is a rocking granny, no doubt about that. Supposedly, her high fashion legs are insured for a million dollars. My whole life is only insured for $500 US in a penny policy my mother took out when I was a toddler. I am sure Tina delivers. In the TV promo, she says with a husky voice and come-on smile, "You want action? I'll give you some action."

Despite the promotion, the tickets for her show were moving very slowly; 200 Rand is serious money for ordinary South Africans. I did not go. Kathleen Bethel did, in the pouring rain. She said the stadium had a good crowd but was still only half-full. It was a predominately white audience. With her blond hair, four-inch heels, short-short dresses, and a stage backdrop filled with lights, glitz, and electronic music, she was packaged for a US audience. It is a matter of taste, but I suspect with Sibongile I got a lot more for less, and not because she outweighed Tina by quite a few pounds!

Speaking of weighty matters, South African TV is introducing body beautiful commercials. "Have the body you always wanted!" Then someone takes out an all-purpose exercise machine that can be folded and stored so you never need to go to a gym. The newscasters and announcers are all slim, all dressed in Western suits and styles, with their hair and faces heavily made up. Even at the bottom of a newscast, there is always an ad, like "Dressed by John Orr." It is as though they are talking about mannequins. The South African woman that you meet every day is often large. I have heard Clementine, who gets on her knees to wash our floors in the biology department, and Royal, who stands on her feet all day washing and ironing clothes at the laundromat, say how they have to go on a diet. Beauty to them is Carly on *Days of Our Lives*. What is wrong with this picture?

Student Protests—April 24 and April 25

On Wednesday, April 24, there was a meeting scheduled in one of the downstairs conference rooms at the university library. The new South African government is in the process of writing a policy paper on biodiversity for approval later during the year. Two government representatives went to various sites, including the universities, to explain how anyone could take part in reviewing the document and giving comments.

I was the first one to show up because I had been working in the library at the time. Sue Higgins, who teaches anatomy at the Medical School, was organizing coffee and cookies outside the door to the meeting room. People began to file in. Then we were told the reason for their lateness. The students were marching again, and some of the people could not get to the library. All the campus buildings were locked. If I had to be locked in, I thought a library was a good place for detainment. In the library, I had lots of books, clean restrooms, and even a very small supply of sugar cookies. So, I went to get a couple of books—Einstein's book on *The Evolution of Physics*, another on sub-atomic particles, and a third on African wildlife. Then I sat and read or skimmed. The meeting finally started. When I left the library, I could see some of the damage to the campus, including smashed windows at the library entrance. Some of the damage was caused by bricks. Later someone said there had also been a bullet hole through the glass.

The next day, I went to 9 a.m. Mass. When I drove back to the security gate at the university at about 9:45, the guard stopped me. He said there was a red alert and the students were marching again. All approaching cars were turned back. I could not go to my office or flat. Instead, I drove to Musgrave shopping center and went to a movie. I had already seen *Jumanji* in St. Louis with Uncle Tom and Aunt Mary. At first, they were not interested in seeing it because Robin Williams was starring. Since I was leaving shortly for Africa, though, they agreed to be taken (or taken in) by me one more time.

The movie is about a game board that comes to life. There were great scenes of rampaging rhinos, zebras, and elephants; monkeys going berserk in kitchens and stores; a lion chase; tropical vines and plants growing out of control and taking over a house; and an indoor monsoon that spills over into the street, along with the crocodiles. Those were good African motifs! Compared to all that mayhem, what was going on at the University of Natal that afternoon was mischief. When I returned to a much quieter campus later in the day, I showed my ID badge and was waved through the security gate.

Later in the week, I was trying to drive my car down a university road that was covered by a dozen or two African students. As I slowly moved forward, they parted like the Red Sea. I rolled down my window, smiled, and said, "I thought you guys were marching again!" They laughed. Anna told the King of Siam that whistling was a great anecdote for fear. Humor is an even better one!

Sickness and Symphonies—April 26 to May 1

I was sick with a very bad cold. This was the first time I had any illness since I arrived in Africa. Maybe these are different cold germs than I have encountered in the US, so they hit me hard. On April 29, I did manage to walk over to a free afternoon concert at the Student Union given by the Natal Philharmonic Orchestra. It was only a five-minute walk from my flat. I arrived early because I thought it might be crowded. As it turned out, only about half the seats were taken. Symphony music does not appeal to a majority of black African students, and I can understand that. For one thing, they usually are not exposed to it. It is not part of their culture. It is part of white culture, Western culture. All the musicians in the orchestra, for example, are white. Many of them are immigrants. The symphony leader is from Russia.

You might see the same result if the St. Louis Symphony gave a noon concert at St. Louis University. Perhaps symphony music does not appeal to most young people, white or black. I do not know. I do know that, from what I have heard of African music, I like it very much. When you hear a group sing, even an impromptu group walking around campus, there is this wonderful harmony. It sounds like singing in parts, but very blended parts. To me, it is nothing like Western choral music.

Guard Dogs

Cyprian, the university security guard, told me that another dog was taken to the hospital. This time it is Rea, the one who would sit for me and jump. He repeated how the guards kick the dogs and how they are not allowed to give them food or water while the dogs are on duty. I called the SPCA myself. The inspector's name was Roland. I told him I am hopeful something will be done this time because Roland is my brother's name too. He promised to try. I offered to buy Rea for Cyprian if the kennel will sell her. Cyprian is just torn up about this.

First, he was attached to Smokey, and then Smokey died. Neither of us wants to see Rea die too from mistreatment.

Riot in Durban—May 4

Six thousand Zulus marched in downtown Durban. They were protesting a ban on carrying their traditional weapons. For the Zulus, the traditional weapons are shields and fighting sticks. The fighting sticks look like long walking sticks with a round knob on top. On this particular day, the tradition was updated; some in the crowd (whether marchers or observers) were carrying AK-47 rifles. Shooting broke out. The headlines in the Durban and Johannesburg papers the next day read: "Durban City Centre Was Like Beirut" and "Durban in Chaos." No one knows where all this is heading.

Johannesburg has the highest murder rate of any city in the world.[25] Of the countries that report statistics on violent crime, South Africa comes in at the top of the list. Only those countries at war, like Bosnia, have citizens more threatened. Somehow you learn to live with that reality. However, it is always there at the back of your mind. After the riot, there was talk on the TV of the government declaring a state of emergency in KwaZulu Natal. Local elections are coming up on June 26. A lot of the violence is part of an ongoing power play between the African National Congress (Mandela's party) and the Inkatha Freedom Party (Chief Buthelezi's party) for political and economic control of this province. It has always been one of the quandaries of any liberation philosophy or movement. How do you liberate hearts and minds? How do you keep the liberated person from becoming an oppressor?

---

[25] In 2021 and 2022, St. Louis, Missouri had the highest murder rate in the US. Sometimes with familiarity, you can become oblivious to danger. Put 9000 miles between you and home and suddenly you are on alert. According to statistics from the United Nations Office on Drugs and Crime, the murder rate in Johannesburg now ranks 9th in the world.

Oribi Gorge—May 4

Fortunately, while the riot was going on, I was in Oribi Gorge. Maybe it was my guardian angel's doing! The gorge is a two-hour drive south of Durban. I made a day trip, starting on Saturday morning and returning that evening. It was on my return that I saw the police cars in downtown Durban and was waved onto a detour. Later I found out why.

The drive through Oribi Gorge was beautiful. Often the road wound beneath a thick canopy of trees and vines. It was as though I had the place to myself. No other cars were in sight. The gorge is about 16 miles long, 3 miles wide, and 1300 feet deep. While that does not approach the size of the Grand Canyon, Oribi is lovely in its own right. Outside the national park, there are private lands that visitors can drive on for a fee. First, I had lunch in the garden at the Oribi Gorge Hotel. Of course, I fed part of my delicious tuna salad to Black Jack, the resident cat, and then watched as a horse nonchalantly walked around the tables until someone from the hotel shooed him away. Maybe the horse was looking for a handout like Black Jack seized. From this private land, I also had a good view of Baboon's Castle, Lehr Falls, and other sights. The falls seemed to end in a gentle slow-motion mist. Behind the spray, on the rock face, were tones of green, brown, gray, and cream. Beautiful, that is all I can say!

This is African bush. There are no security railings like you would find in US National Parks. As I stood right on the edge of the precipice, I thought that anyone could come behind me, give me one soft push or one startling shout, and I would be free-falling into this chasm. It is wonderful though to see all this without man-made railings, concrete steps, and explanatory signs.

The day at the gorge was very hot. At each viewing site, there was a guard to assist visitors. I am sure the hotel does not pay them much. One was using his machete to cut down tall grass. When I came back from viewing the falls, I saw him resting under a tree and sharpening his machete. I thanked him and gave him 20 Rand. He thanked me with his eyes and smile. He could not speak English. I just feel the need to help the people I meet in some way. Most of them have so little. It is not charity but justice. I know I cannot change the system by myself but I have to do what I can. Every time you go out, you pass squatter camps, street kids begging for money, or a mother sitting on the sidewalk with two or three small children. It hurts. It is supposed to.

Truth and Reconciliation Commission—May 7 to May 10

The Truth and Reconciliation Commission (TRC) came to Durban for four days of hearings. Archbishop Desmond Tutu was the chairman. The purpose of the Commission is to allow the victims and families, who suffered during 46 years of apartheid, to come forward and tell their stories. A record of this pain will be compiled as a history lesson for the new South Africa. Hopefully, those who have suffered will unburden their grief. By telling their stories to a nationwide audience, they can receive support and empathy from listeners.

There is controversy surrounding the TRC. Some do not believe those who tortured, murdered, and shattered families and lives should be granted amnesty. Others are cynical and doubt that the TRC can do anything to make real reparation. The TRC cannot guarantee that a mother who lost her son will receive a pension because she no longer has a son to provide for her as she ages. The TRC cannot guarantee that children will receive scholarships for school because they have lost one or more parents and live with relatives that are hard-pressed to even feed them or clothe them. The TRC cannot guarantee that victims of torture will receive medical and psychiatric treatment. In some small way, though, many people think that the TRC can help to bring reconciliation without revenge.

Tickets were required to attend the hearings. I called the US Information Service and they arranged for me to have a ticket for each day the TRC was in Durban. The hearings were held at the

Durban Jewish Center. Desmond Tutu remarked that this was unin-tentionally appropriate since the Jewish people had suffered so much and had been trying to heal from the Holocaust for 50 years. The Commission wanted to hold the hearings at the Mahatma Gandhi Memorial Building. Durban and its surrounding areas are where Gandhi spent 22 years of his life and where he became a political activist for non-violence. Ironically, that building was considered too big of a security problem. There were bomb threats and other expec-tations of violence. After the recent riots, I was a little nervous about going to the hearings. In my heart, though, I felt if people dared to come and tell their stories, others must have the courage to come and listen.

Visitors went through a security check at the front door of the DJC, but no one could seriously believe that would protect anyone if a person or group was intent on setting off a bomb. On first entering the building, I saw Desmond Tutu in a corner chatting with a few people. I walked toward him, hoping to say hello and shake his hand, but I did not want to intrude. Instead, I stopped about six feet away (frozen in place!), and simply watched. That in itself was a gift. When Tutu turned to go into the auditorium, I melted and followed behind. Fortunately, I found a seat in the third row, center aisle, behind the press seats. That became my seat for the next four days.[26] Each day I watched as Tutu shook the hands of those who were going to testify and greeted the press. He is known for saying, "Just call me Arch."

The horror stories that unfolded were difficult to hear. One woman, Mrs. Helen Kearney, was a very good storyteller. When she was in high school, she prepared to be a secretary, but upon gradua-tion decided to run away and join the circus. For many years she was a trapeze artist. Eventually, she settled down and worked behind the bar at a popular restaurant called Magoo's. She took the job because she enjoyed people; working behind the bar, she became a friend,

[26] One day someone called to tell me that I was on the evening news. There was a close shot of me watching the proceedings. I was oblivious. It appeared that I was concen-trating, which I was!

psychiatrist, and confessor to her customers. They became family to her. She was working in the bar one night when a bomb exploded. The only thing that saved her was that she was in the process of walking from one room to the next and was beneath reinforced steel and brickwork. When she turned around, she spoke of seeing half a head, large splinters of glass sticking out of bodies, human flesh and blood all over the walls—and she smelled burning skin and death. Two of her teenage daughters just missed the bombing by minutes. They had stopped by the bar after a date to tell their mother goodnight, just as they always did on weekends. The bomb was planted by a man named Robert McBride. He is now in the South African parliament and is the deputy director of Foreign Affairs. Mrs. Kearney only asked for help for the surviving victims and that men like McBride "who have no godliness" not be able to hold public office.

Another woman told of the death of her son, Stompie. This is a famous case in South Africa. Stompie was only fourteen years old when he was killed. Winnie Mandela was convicted of his earlier kidnapping and assault. Winnie is the ex-wife of Nelson Mandela, the president of South Africa. The divorce went through this year. The whole affair received almost as much publicity as Britain's Diana and Charles.

There was an eleven-year-old child at the hearings, Phoenix Meyer, who was a year old when her parents were killed. Her mother, Jacqui, was white and her father was black. That is why they were murdered. Jacqui's parents testified at the hearings. Among other things they said that their daughter "died for lovely people." They saw their daughter's death in the context of black Africans' struggle for freedom. What a remarkable place to have arrived in their grief! "I want our society to redevelop the moral attitude that to kill another human being is a totally and absolutely unacceptable sin," Jacqui's mother said. "I want our country to be a place that never again allows people to damage the lives of others—especially not because of their color or because of their living belief in justice and goodness—which is ultimately why Jacqui was killed."

There were tales of prisoners being pushed out of prison windows to their deaths; tales of men whose genitals were hooked up to electrical wires and men who had to get their drinking water from the flush toilet; tales of torture; tales of murder; tales of fear. When I first went to the hearings, I thought it was going to be all about the crimes of white against black. We quickly learned that everyone was involved in the killing—white, black, Indian, and colored. Desmond Tutu said that the whole country had been "embraced by evil" under apartheid.[27]

Lights Out—May 12

My electricity was turned off unexpectedly on Sunday at about 8 a.m. I was worried about the food in my freezer. First, I asked the parish priest for help because I thought there might be a freezer in the parish hall with some space. He hesitated to reply. "That's okay," I said. "I realize your job is to take care of our spiritual needs, not our frozen foods!" He laughed. Then I called Pat and Norman Berjak in the biology department. Pat told me to use the freezer in the biology lab. I said, "Pat, I don't want to open the freezer door and see some monkey in a Ziploc bag or some crocodile with a frozen grin!" She assured me that this particular freezer only had plant seeds. So, I packed up my car trunk (or boot, as they say here) with food from my refrigerator and headed over to the biology department. It turned out to be a godsend since the electricity did not go on until late in the evening.

I spent most of the day with Pat and Norman, feeding the birds in their backyard and then making a trip to see Norman's father. As it turned out, he was not at home. The pensioner left a note on his door—"Gone out to dinner." His guests sat in the garden and

---

[27] I was blessed to be part of this historic event in South Africa. The new Constitution of the Republic of South Africa was adopted on 8 May 1996, approved by the Constitutional Court on 4 December 1996, and took effect on 4 December 1997. My experience in South Africa gives me hope as my own country continues to struggle with issues of race and ethnicity as well as the necessary limitations on freedom even in a democracy.

wondered what he was up to and with whom. Good for him! Finally we departed, none the wiser.

Twin Streams and Ian Garland—May 13

Michael Berjak and I drove up to Mtuzini. This is where Ian Garland's home is. Twin Streams is about 175 km north of Durban and way off the beaten track. You drive for miles, over dirt roads and through forest. We took a cellular phone with us this trip, in case we had car trouble.

I will be working with Ian and his Zulu assistant, Jobe Mafuleka, to gather information about local trees and plants. Ian is very well-known here. When Peter Raven, from the Missouri Botanical Garden, was in South Africa several years ago, Ian showed him a site with rare South African flora.[28] Raven wrote a letter to the government stressing how important it was to preserve the site. After learning I was from St. Louis, Ian relayed that story. He thought I might know Peter Raven. I told him that I only knew his considerable reputation.

Ian lives with his wife, Jean, and two large tan dogs, Bess and Rusty. They are in the home that belonged to his father, when all the land was still a sugar cane farm. For fifty years, Ian rehabilitated the land with indigenous trees. In the process, he created a "heritage site" for South Africa.

We reached the house at about 3:30 p.m. As a result, very little work got done that day. Ian took us on a short one-hour walk around the property, showing off his beloved trees as usual. He reminded me a bit of Uncle Jay. When I brought a visitor to Ironton, Uncle Jay immediately had to take us on a tour of his house and his stone wall. Each stone in that wall was pulled from the earth and stacked. We had dinner and a little conversation before Ian and Jean headed to bed. Michael and I stayed up to watch a videotape of David Attenborough's *Life of a Plant*.

---

[28] Peter Raven was born 13 June 1936 in Shanghai, China. Currently, he is the President Emeritus of the Missouri Botanical Garden.

I was the first one up the next morning at about 5 a.m. Ian and I went out in his pickup truck around 5:30. The back was filled with African school children. They were children of some of the workers on the farm. As we drove them to school, Ian pointed out different things. We saw a southern banded snake eagle, which Ian said was very rare. At one point, we passed a straight line of trees which I assumed was planted by hand or maybe by a cultivator. Ian said that line of trees was planted naturally. There had been a fence there. The birds used to feed on nearby fruit and then come sit on the fence. Eventually, the birds digested their breakfast and got down to business at this aviary latrine. This is how the trees all were planted in a straight line.

After we dropped off the children, Ian showed me where a new highway was coming through. Then he went back and loaded up the pickup with a hundred seedlings. We delivered them to the men in the field for planting—just like a regular Johnny Appleseed. Ian and I had put in a morning's work before the rest in the house were up.

Michael and I spent the rest of the day following Ian around his farm, while Ian pointed out different trees. Ian is in his seventies, but Michael and I were hard-pressed to keep up with him. At one point, we had to cross this old rickety bridge. Michael was following behind Ian and I was following behind Michael. Both of them forgot to tell me to walk near the sides of the bridge, not down the middle. When I came within about fifteen feet of shore, a bridge slat gave way. My left leg fell so fast through the hole that my body did not have time to tense up. Ian and Michael were frantic. With my butt on the floor of the bridge and one leg dangling though a hole, I was laughing. Of course, I was lucky that the broken wood did not skin my entire leg. Ian and Michael stayed on shore. I had to get out of this predicament by myself, and I did—much to my surprise! I guess I am stronger than I think.

After that bit of excitement, we just carried on looking at more trees. On the way back, we had to pass over the same bridge. Because there were no railings, I held Michael's shirt tail for balance and walked on the outer side of the bridge. As we were walking, I told Michael that we were like parading elephants, with me holding the tail of the pachyderm in front. This time I made it across without an accident.

When we returned to the farm, Michael and I interviewed Ian on tape about the site itself and how he restored it to indigenous woodland. Ian surprised us with the news that he and his wife were moving to Durban at the end of August. He did not want to return home someday to find his wife murdered. "We are being hunted," Ian said. "I have an appreciation for the brutality of the blacks, the brutality of underprivileged people."

It took me by surprise to hear Ian say that because I have seen him with Jobe. Ian has great respect and affection for him. Even so, I know Ian feels threatened and frustrated now, and that is making him angry. He is apparently from a wealthy background. Two of the oldest and most expensive private schools in South Africa are Michaelhouse (1896) and Hilton College (1872). Ian went to one and his brother to the other. The schools are called the Eton of South Africa.

You ANC Nothing Yet—May 15

I went to the Sneddon Theatre to see Pieter Dirk Uys. He is a local comedian. In the first ten minutes of the show, he had to mention every four-letter word he knew in the eleven South African languages. After he got that out of the way, he went on to satirize everybody on the South African scene—zipping off one costume and zipping up another. His cast of characters included the new South African voter ("I want a job. I want a house. I want your car."); the old Afrikaner with all his prejudices showing; Nelson Mandela and Winnie Mandela ("the rebel without a Xhosa"); Desmond Tutu with both hands covered with rings ("Oh, my darlings, oh, my dears."). His best-known character is a wealthy white Jewish woman, Evita, who now wears a sequined dress that looks like the ANC flag. The real-life Mandela has a picture on his desk of him and Evita (Peter in drag). Desmond Tutu asked Uys to put him in the show. He was the first black African that Uys satirized. Beneath all this, Uys is also making fun of himself—as a white Jewish gay Afrikaner. His political humor is very popular. "It's terrible, you can't even find a cardboard box in South Africa anymore," he whined. "They've all been used for houses." For a TV special, he did practically the same show for an all-black African audience. They laughed right along with him. The times are changing in South Africa.

Giant's Castle—May 19

Giant's Castle Game Reserve supposedly has about 40% of the rock art discovered in South Africa. At Bushmen's Cave, there are approximately 700 rock paintings. When I heard that, I made up my mind to go. I drove up on a Saturday. Unfortunately, I underestimated how long it would take to get there. Once you turn off the highway and onto dirt roads, the going is slow. By the time I got to Giant's Castle, it was late in the afternoon. I started for Bushmen's Cave. Halfway there, the sky darkened and the thunder rolled. So, I headed back to the car. The scenery coming and going was still beautiful. The reserve is right in the middle of the Drakensberg Mountains. Going home was a challenge. The rain turned the dirt roads into mudslides. For 40 km, I did not see a person or a car in sight. Half the time I thought I was driving a tractor because the ruts in the road were so deep. I will be going back for the rock paintings. Next time though, I will book ahead for overnight accommodation in the park.

Muti Market—May 29

I went to the muti market with Dehn and two of the Zulu technicians in the biology department, Mjuba and Herbert. At the muti market, black Africans buy and sell plants, roots, and herbs that are used in traditional healing. Dehn and I were the only white persons there. This is not a place where tourists go.

Someone from the biology department goes to the muti market every week, gathering information on the plants that are sold and asking the women (yes, the sellers are almost exclusively women) about the plants. Are they poisonous? Are they rare? What illnesses are they used for? Mjuba pointed out one of the sangomas (traditional healers) who was buying muti. She was dressed in this beautiful African caftan that was bright blue, black, and white. On the front and back of the caftan was the pattern of a large crocodile. Around her head was a matching cloth wound in a turban. She looked very well-off. Some of the sangomas make more money than the MDs!

The women who were selling the muti were a real contrast. All around them was a mountain of garbage—plastic bottles, plastic wrappers, bits of paper, old tires, you name it. Women sat with their babies, nursing them, changing diapers, feeding them. Sometimes a mother would put her infant on the ground and go to talk to a customer, but the women nearby obviously kept an eye on the baby. Like the African proverb says, "It takes a village to raise a child." I saw a woman use sunflowers to sweep her little patch of earth, then spread a cloth out, and place her plants neatly in rows. In the background, there was a pot of something cooking; it must have been lunch.

At one end of the market was a makeshift shack with a few boards and a tin roof held down by bricks. This was where the man stayed who was in charge of the market. Dehn had to get his permission to talk to the women. Dehn also brought a camera with him. He would take pictures of the women and their children. You could see them straightening their clothes and the hair of their babies before posing for the picture. When Dehn comes back the following week, he will give out the pictures. This may be the only picture these women ever have of themselves and their children. It is just another way of building goodwill.

While we were going around to the women, Mjuba came across

a plant that the biology department did not have as yet. He asked the woman selling the plant what it was used for. Then he tried to translate from Zulu to English for Dehn and me. "It's used for when you want to communicate with your ancestors," he said. "You burn it and . . . I don't know how to explain." I said, "Is it like incense that rises and takes your prayers to the ancestors?" Mjuba got excited. "That's it, Doris," Mjuba said as he grabbed me. "We must bring you every time we come here." Inside, I thought, "You're not the only one who practices an ancient religion, Mjuba!"

We did not go to the animal muti market. I was glad. As sentimental as I am about animals, I did not want to see animal parts spread out on the ground, like the eye of a newt and the toe of a baboon. Maybe that is what was boiling in the lunch pot! Parts are parts, as KFC's competitors say.

St. Lucia, Mkuze, and Hluhluwe—May 31

I drove up the north coast for a weekend of scenery and animals. It was about a three-hour drive to St. Lucia, the largest freshwater lagoon in Southern Africa. Four rivers feed into the lake, the most important being the Mkuze in the north. For about $12 US, I took a two-hour boat ride on the lake, from 2:30 to 4:30 p.m. The sun was in my eyes on the way out, but I still managed to see about a dozen or so bathing hippos, as well as some reedbuck. A reedbuck is an antelope that lies in the reeds near the water's edge. They are very difficult to spot through the trees. There were various water birds and one fish eagle, as well. One of the men sitting near me found out I was an American and he talked to me at length. He asked about Clinton, about Desert Storm, even about farmers. It was like being on *Meet the Press*.[29]

That night I stayed in the Boma Hotel. The person at the Natal Parks Board Office, who sold me the boat ticket, recommended it.

---

[29] *Meet the Press* has been on American TV since 6 November 1945. It is a program with news and interviews focused mainly on politics, foreign policy, and economics.

The smallest accommodation was two bedrooms, two full baths, a living room, bar, and fully furnished kitchen (including a microwave), all for about $44 US. My second-floor balcony faced trees, gray-and-white monkeys, and a small patch of the lake.

For dinner, I went to the nearby Lakeview Restaurant. The restaurant opened at 6 p.m. and I was their first and only early customer. In South Africa, dinner is usually between 7-9 p.m. Thirty minutes later I still had only a Coca-Cola and a piece of bread. Service was slow, but, when the food did arrive, it was delicious. I had Kingklip covered in cheese, mushroom, and shrimp sauce. On the side were a baked potato and a salad with shredded Roquefort cheese on top. After weeks of eating my non-cooking, it was a treat.

When I went back to my room, I watched *Sunday Bloody Sunday*, one of the old movie classics. I also watched a late-night Oprah show about how easy it is to break into a house. After that, I did not sleep very well on my nice firm double bed; I kept thinking about how easy it would be to slip a knife into the sliding glass doors and open them. I am not sure if I thought the monkeys were armed with switchblades or what!

Saturday morning, I drove to Mkuze. Again, it was a couple of hours drive because I was traveling over dirt roads. I spent about four hours at Mkuze, just driving through the park, looking for animals, and finding some. In the afternoon, I headed further north to Hluhluwe Game Park. Unlike Mkuze, Hluhluwe is very hilly. It is a beautiful place and has been a wildlife sanctuary since 1897. That makes it one of the first in South Africa. I was tired when I drove into the reserve because I had been driving all day on very bad dirt roads. It was about 4:00 p.m. and the sun was starting to go down. Two cars were parked across the dirt road that led to Hilltop, the place where I had a reservation in the park for the night. I knew the people in the cars must be looking at animals, but I was anxious to check into my cabin. One of the cars pulled over to let me by. I had only gone about twenty feet when I saw the reason the cars had been parked. There was a huge male elephant at the edge of the road stripping leaves from a tree. I moved my car to the opposite side of the road and thought I could just creep by him. That was a very dumb move.

When I advanced about another ten yards, the elephant charged out of the bush and came right for my VW. He had two long ivory tusks. Raising his head, he trumpeted loudly. I threw the car in reverse, backed up, and stopped. The elephant stopped, raised his head again, trumpeted, and ran right for me. He had drawn a line in the dirt and I was over it! As fast as I could, I backed up again and he came at me. I had seen the movie *Jumanji* where the elephant walks right over the car; that image flashed before my mind. Quickly, I realized those tusks were long enough to protrude over the front hood and through the windshield. Believe me, it was scary! The elephant finally trumpeted again and went back to his tree. This time I left him to eat uninterrupted.

The next day when I was checking out of the reserve, a man came up to me. He said, "What did you think of that elephant yesterday?" I responded with surprise, "Were you there?" "I was in one of the cars," he replied. "The elephant was very aggressive." Then the man offered another insight. "I thought you must be pretty excited," he said. I told him the worst part was that I did not even get a picture of the elephant. My camera was on the front seat, but I needed my free hand on the gear shift. Would you believe that was the only elephant I saw for the rest of my stay in the park! Luckily, in retrospect, it was up-close and personal!

The hut that I rented in the park was very large with a modern bathroom. It had a beautiful high thatched roof with thick poles holding it up. There are no keys to the room. When you leave your hut, you leave it open. There are, however, locks on the inside of the door.

That evening I had a delicious meal at the park restaurant (Kingklip again), and then I went on a three-hour night drive through the park. It was a tour and cost 50 Rand, a little over $10 US. The only drawback was that it was raining and cold, and we were in an open truck. Half of the tourists were Americans. Five of the tourists were small children, so we did not exactly take many animals by surprise.

I am sure they could hear us a mile away. The children wanted to operate the lights that were used to scan the bush. So sometimes the light was in the trees and sometimes on the ground. At one point, a German tourist simply wrested the light away from one of the children. He was trying to take night pictures and was frustrated that now the light was on the animal and, oops, now it was not.

The father and grandparents of the children kept telling them how wonderful they were doing, what keen eyes they had, and how smart they were. They must have been to Child Psychology 101, or watched a few Oprah shows about building esteem. No matter, I just sat huddled in the rain, with my purple jacket on, my arms crossed, and my hands in my armpits trying to keep warm. Once in a while, I spotted some animals, and the tour driver stopped. Of course, nobody told me what keen eyes I had. The over-ten crowd has to build their own self-esteem! At the river, our spotlight picked up a swimming crocodile. That is when the German tourist stood up in the truck and grabbed the spotlight, muttering something guttural.

By the time I returned to my room, I was very wet and very tired. I wanted to get up at 5 a.m. to go out again looking for animals, but I knew my body probably would not comply. Instead, I set the alarm on my watch for 8 a.m. and went to bed.

Sometime later, I heard a voice distinctly say, "Doris." I woke up and said out loud, "Okay." The room was dark. I threw my legs over the side of the bed, turned on the light, and looked at my watch. It read 4:59:50 a.m. I have no explanation for the voice at all. My alarm was still set for 8 a.m. In my head, I heard: "I have a gift to give you." Quickly, I dressed and used my flashlight to walk up the sloping path to my car.

It was so dark that, apart from the flashlight, I could not see where I was going. When I reached the car, I started the ignition, put my headlights on, and went hunting for animals. Amazingly, I found them. On one stretch of empty road, a rhino practically walked right in front of my car as he was crossing the road. He looked right at me. Later I saw a giraffe family right by the road—mother, father, and baby. On the other side of the road, two giraffes were wrapping their necks around each other. It was wonderful to be out there searching by myself with no voices, no cars. With light gradually breaking, my view of the sky and earth was a gift.

I spent the rest of the day driving around Hluhluwe and then took the narrow corridor into the adjoining Umfolozi game reserve. The three-day weekend was wonderful.

The Other Archbishop—June 5

I met Archbishop Denis Hurley today.[30] The pastor at my church put me in touch with him. When he initially phoned me, he said he had been in St. Louis once. He remembered some German had been archbishop then. I said, "Ritter." Immediately, he replied with enthusiasm, "That's right!" The current archbishop came up in the conversation, and I could not remember his name. Archbishop Hurley coaxed, "It's something Italian, like Rigatoni." A voice from childhood suddenly popped in my head, "Macaroni full of baloney." Finally, it came to me—Rigali. Fortunately, I passed that test.

Archbishop Hurley lives in a rectory adjacent to a downtown church, Emmanuel Cathedral. The parking lot is enclosed by a black

---

[30] When I first met Archbishop Denis Hurley, he introduced himself as "the other archbishop" because Archbishop Desmond Tutu was more widely known and more highly awarded. His youth was spent on Robben Island; his father was the lighthouse keeper. Robben Island is where Nelson Mandela spent eighteen years in prison. In 1946, he became a bishop at 31, the youngest in the ranks at that time. As bishop, he wasted no time condemning apartheid as evil. In 1951, he became an archbishop. Ten years later, he was assigned to a commission charged with making the preparations for the Second Vatican Council. When Pope John XXIII convened the Council on 11 October 1962, Archbishop Hurley contributed to commissions on seminaries and Catholic education. He called the Council "the greatest project of adult education ever held in the world." His last article was in *The Southern Cross: The Catholic Magazine of Southern Africa* (17 December 2003). The whole universe was his focus. Archbishop Hurley wrote that in the Big Bang and the unfolding of the universe over billions of years "God is present, sustaining, upholding, promoting, and perfecting." Archbishop Hurley died on 13 February 2004, at the age of 89.

iron fence in what was an old cemetery. Some of the original head-stones are there, generally those for priests and nuns who died in late 1800 and early 1900. Out of curiosity, I asked Archbishop Hurley what they did with the other bodies when they installed the parking lot. I thought they might have paved right over them—maybe not a highway to heaven, but a back parking lot for paradise. He said there was not much left of the bodies; you could scoop up about a dozen of them in a little box. That is not as poetic as Shakespeare's words about "dusty death" but his thoughts were along the same lines.

From a tour of the church, I learned that Archbishop Hurley spoke English, Zulu, Italian, and French. A sign outside his confessional said so. He is also the chairman of the Committee on AIDS. The reason for my visit was to let him know that I wanted to volunteer. While I am not sure how I can help, I know that between nothing and everything, there is something I can do. He said he would make some contacts for me.

Tomorrow I am going to a seminar in the biology department on the "HIV Epidemic in Southern Africa." Conservative estimates are that 25% of the South African population has AIDS. Bishop Napier said that, of all the people dying in one of the large public hospitals in Durban, half are dying of AIDS. It is really scary.

Archbishop Hurley is also going to put me in touch with some of the people working at the squatter camps. He asked me what we call such camps in the US. I told him we do not have squatter camps. Do we have public housing, ghettos, and homelessness? Yes. However, the closest thing to a squatter camp was when Larry Rice, a preacher and founder of the New Life Evangelistic Center, put up cardboard boxes in the front yard of St. Louis City Hall as an overnight protest and homeless campout.

At the rectory, they referred to the archbishop as "Your Grace." I asked him if he had seen the movie *Saving Grace*. It is about a relatively young cardinal (age 57) who reluctantly becomes pope. He is followed around by two cardinal aides all day long. The pope is constantly hearing, "Yes, Your Holiness" and "No, Your Holiness." The pope tells them that he does not want to be called Holiness. One cardinal says privately to the other, "What does he want us to call him—Your Mediocrity?" Day after day, that cardinal nervously mumbles new titles to himself, looking for something to call this man who dislikes the trappings of his new office: Your Magnificence, Your Superbness, Your Humbleness. Archbishop Hurley laughed heartily, but perhaps he made a mental note: radical Catholic.

Another bit of news, Archbishop Desmond Tutu retired this week. He was asked what he was going to do now. "Sleep and read," he replied. "I like a rum and coke, and if you bring me a tub of rum raisin ice cream, you'll be my friend for life." Then he gave that giggle he is famous for. He is alright!

AIDS in South Africa—June 5

A virologist at University of Natal Medical School gave a seminar today on "The AIDS Epidemic in South Africa." He said KwaZulu Natal, the province where I live, is the "epicenter" of the AIDS epidemic in South Africa. In April 1996, he analyzed blood from all the patients that went through the mortuary at King Edward Hospital, which is about a five-minute drive from where I live. The virologist found that 51.8% of all the patients who had died at the hospital that month had HIV.[31] He also took blood samples from the female patients coming to the Durban Neonatal Center. Almost 25% of them had AIDS. He used a very unscientific term to describe the results of his tests: frightening. Who would disagree with him?

An interesting point though, one of the traditional healers told the virologist that he could cure AIDS. This is not unusual. Other healers have claimed the same thing. The virologist told the healer that he (the healer) did not even know if these patients had AIDS, so he could not know if he was curing them. The virologist told the

---

[31] HIV and AIDS are different but closely linked. HIV is a virus that can lead to a condition called AIDS. AIDS is sometimes referred to as stage 3 HIV.

healer to send these patients that he thought had AIDS to him, and he would test them. The healer did and, according to the virologist, almost all of them had HIV.

The virologist does not believe the healer can cure AIDS. Still, he does believe that some of the traditional herbs and plants that are used to treat sick people do help them to continue to work and lead a reasonably normal life. For example, the healer was able to cure a woman's case of shingles which was even more painful and threatening because of her HIV infection. The doctor said he is no longer willing to just dismiss the claims of the traditional healers. He is asking for research money to follow up on it. In the United States, he said, we can prolong the productive life of HIV patients for ten or fifteen years through various drugs. Africa cannot afford these drugs, but the virologist feels that maybe the traditional healers can play a similar role with their herbal medicine. My work with the Indigenous Plant Usage Program may take me deeper into contact with the traditional healers. I would like that.

African TV Guide

For the couch potatoes, here is a list of American TV programs on South African TV this week: *CNN, Dennis the Menace, America's Funniest Home Videos, Roseanne, Cheers, Adventures of Tom Sawyer, Seinfeld, Days of Our Lives, Bold and the Beautiful, American Gothic, Larry King Live, Oprah Winfrey, Santa Barbara, Young and the Restless, Murder She Wrote, Mad About You, Tales from the Crypt, Touched by an Angel, Rescue 911, New York Undercover, The Cosby Show, Due South, Kurt Vonnegut's Monkey House, Star Trek: Voyager, Jag, Space Precinct, Faerie Tale Theatre, The Cosby Mysteries, The Commish, The Jeff Foxworthy Show.* There are also shows that never made it beyond one season, like *Madman of the People.* That tells you something about the American culture that is being exported to Africa. We also have M-Net, a movie network that you have to pay for and own a decoder to access. I do not. Tonight, for example, they are showing Jack Nicholson in *Wolf* and also in *Hoffa*. In South Africa, you are supposed to buy a TV license for viewing any station. If you do not have a TV license, it is punishable by six months in prison and a fine of 2000 Rand. It is called "TV pirating." I do not have a license. If you ever get a postcard from a South African prison, you will know they caught up with me.

There are three channels in South Africa: SABC1, SABC2, and SABC3. All are government-operated. Each channel advertises programs on all the other channels. SABC3 is the channel for English speakers, although a few English programs are on the other channels as well. To complicate matters, at 6:30 p.m., SABC3 is transmitted over SABC2 and SABC2 is transmitted over SABC3. As a result, you have to physically change the dial at that time to continue getting the programs you expect. Some of the silent intros to the programs are strange. If it is a cops-and-robbers type of show, there is a man with an AK-47 assault rifle on the left side of the screen at the beginning and after each commercial. There are commercials but not quite as many as in the US.

SABC3 has started televising some of the parliament sessions. Someone may be speaking very fervently but, when the camera pans to the MP chairs, hardly anyone is there. This is democracy in action. It seems ironic that the black Africans struggled so long to get to parliament, and now many of them are reluctant to show up. They probably never realized how boring the endless talking and debating can be. I am sure attendance in the US Congress would not hold up to scrutiny either.

Mandela at University of Natal—June 13

The Campaign for Passive Resistance was celebrating a fifty-year effort, commemorated in a new book. That book was on sale in the Student Union at the university. Nelson Mandela was the guest speaker for the celebration. His entrance was supposed to take place at 5 p.m. I headed over to the building at about 4:15 to get a good seat. At the entrance to the Student Union was a large sign of an automatic gun in a red circle with a line through it. Humanity has developed a universal sign for "no guns" just like "no smoking." I went through security; badges and bags were checked.

When I entered the auditorium, I did not realize the seats on the floor were reserved. The next option was nearby stairs, at the top of which was an overlook. There were no chairs set up on the overlook. It was standing room only. Fortunately, I managed to find a space on the far left of the railing. From there, I had a clear view of the stage and podium where Mandela would speak. On my left were some large planters and ferns. Beyond that point were the stairs going down to the main floor. More and more students kept coming to the overlook. As a result, I was getting pushed tighter and tighter into the balcony railing; in fact, my upper body was leaning over it. A female student tried to jam between me and the potted plants and even climb up on one of the planters. Fortunately, there was no room. I said to her, "Be careful you don't fall." She smiled. "I won't fall," she said. "Be free!" As I was almost heading over the railing myself, I said, "How about while we're being free, we be non-violent as well."

The shoving and shouting from the students were getting dangerous. So, I thought "that's it, I'm out of here." Before I could do anything, I was pushed over part of a potted plant and onto my back. Momentum slid me down some of the stairs. My feet were on the upper part of the stairs and my head was further down. The students kept coming up the stairs and jumping over me. It was frightening, your worst nightmare about being in a crowd out of control. I thought for sure I would be trampled. There I was spread upside-down on my back; all I could see were legs leaping over me like jumping gazelle. I covered my head with my arms and yelled, "Stop, for God's sake!" For a second everything stopped. Suddenly, someone from behind had me by the shoulders and another person in front had my arm; they pulled me up so that I was facing the top of the stairs. Two guards tried to hold the crowd while I turned around. When I did, my feet were right on the edge of a step. As I slowly started down the steps to get out of the way, yelling students rushed by me. There was an announcement that the empty seats on the main floor were now open to any visitors.

Finally, I did make it to the ground floor, shaken but unhurt. Immediately, I grabbed the first seat I came to and sat down. After all that happened, at least I would see Mandela. The students went wild when he entered and walked down the middle aisle. They were chanting "Mandiba, Mandela." Mandiba is Nelson Mandela's clan name, culturally more important than his given name. When the students finally quieted down, the program began. We listened to about thirty minutes of other speakers. Then Mandela rose and read his speech. Surprisingly, it was rather dry. I wanted to be there, but I found my mind drifting and caught myself just looking around. Even so, Mandela's name and presence are still magic in South Africa.

At the end of the speech, Mandela put aside the papers and simply spoke. He spoke about those who were afraid of what was going to happen in South Africa "after Mandela." Is there life after Mandela? He told the students they must stand against such fears. When Albert Lutuli, a Nobel Peace Prize winner who spoke for non-violence and human fraternity, was a leader in South Africa, everyone asked the same question. Mandela said that no one knew when Lutuli left that Oliver Tambo, a revered leader against apartheid, would emerge. Mandela was implying that when he left the scene, someone else would arise because an ongoing democracy depends on an organization, not on a man. He also spoke of the need to respect the law. Not even the president, he said, was above the law.[32]

The most attractive thing about Mandela, I think, is his generosity to former enemies and his apparent lack of bitterness. He

---

[32] In revisiting this diary after so many years, I find those statements by Mandela mind-blowing. Today, it is Americans who are facing challenges to our democracy and to respect for law. Some would have us believe that the law does not apply to a President or even to a former President. That is counter to the Constitution of the United States and to the American story since 1789.

mentioned that, when he became president, he appointed a certain judge to a very high position. This was the same judge, he said, who made sure that he spent 27 years in prison. There was only one woman on the stage, and she was white. As Mandela mentioned the judge, she smiled and shook her head in affirmation. Mandela respected the judge's fairness and effort to carry out the law without prejudice. You have to admire Mandela for that quality alone. When you read his autobiography, though, you learn that he had to grow to that grace over the years. If only we could all show patience and just keep working on our humanity. That is what it takes.

Odds and Ends—June 15 to June 17

I drove up to Hilton which is just north of Pietermaritzburg and about a one hour drive from Durban. I went to see Jean Counihan; her sister Claire; Claire's husband, Colin; and Jean's mother. I met Jean back in the 1980s when I came to South Africa on business. We have kept in touch at Christmas time over the years. Jean wanted me to see the house that Claire was building for her next door to her own. Right now, Jean lives in Johannesburg. Claire is a microbiology technician by training. A couple of years ago, she unexpectedly started building houses. She built the Jesuit house near Hilton last year. When she took me by there, no Jesuits were home.

Apparently, in that area there are a whole bunch of religious orders. Hilton is an expensive area. Michaelhouse and Hilton are both nearby. These are the most expensive private schools in South Africa. Jean and Claire took me to see Hilton. It was crowded because there was a rugby match that day. The buildings were in South African Dutch style called Cape Dutch with whitewashed walls. The whole place was dripping money.

The next day, Sunday, I went to a play in downtown Durban called *Old Boys*. It was about boys going to Michaelhouse and then becoming part of the old boy network in South Africa. The play talked about the harassment of younger students, homosexuality, and poor socialization because boys came out of Michaelhouse thinking women were some alien species. It was also about whole families that went to Hilton. "I hate it here," one boy says. "Why did my father send me?" His friend has a quick answer. "Because he went here and he hated it and his father went here and he hated it," the boy says. "That's tradition." Some of the "old boys" were in the audience because I caught their cross-talk during the intermission.

Monday was the Comrades Marathon. It is an 85 km race (approximately 53 miles). One year the race is from Durban to Pietermaritzburg and the next year from Pietermaritzburg to Durban. At 5:45 a.m. about 13,000 runners set out. They have to finish within ten hours for recognition that they were in the race. The winner this year finished in 5 ½ hours. It was a strange sight. One guy had a sign that said, "I'm here for the beer." Another sign said, "Soli Deo Gloria" which means "Glory to God alone." That must have belonged to one of the four missionaries who were registered for the race. In total contrast, a fellow had a super-size condom on his head. Another wore a Simpson mask (not O.J. Simpson but Homer from *The Simpsons*). Two people had rhino costumes. Can you imagine running 85 km in a rhino costume?

One of the rhinos did finish under the ten-hour limit. The other rhino might have been snatched as he went by Lion Park because I do not think he reached the finish line. When TV showed the last people to make it over the finish line before the ten-hour deadline, it was incredible. They could hardly move, much less run. One guy scooted over on his butt. Another was pushed over the line because he could not go any further. Even the winners could hardly walk up the steps to get their awards five hours later. Many came down the steps backward, their legs straight out. A Russian, Dmitri Grishin, took top prize in the men's category and an American, Ann Trason, in the women's category. Trason led her challengers all the way and finished about forty minutes behind Grishin. She broke the previous female record by almost twenty minutes. Ironically, Trason said she felt bad the entire race, from start to finish.

Nelson Mandela gave out the gold medals and other awards, along with a hug for the winners, male and female. He is loved here. If I thought I could walk 85 km in ten hours, I would have tried, because the guy who came in last before the cut-off gun sounded received a big trophy and a hug from Mandela as well. He said he only trained for the marathon by walking about 100 km the entire year. That is like walking to and from your parking lot every day.

Before the race, I went to morning Mass at the OMI Provincial House. Since it is only a few blocks from the university, it is convenient. I called the adjacent convent the night before to see if there would be Mass and talked to one of the African nuns, Sister Gertrude. She said, "Yes, Father doesn't take a holiday." I told her, "Well, I thought he might be running in the Comrades." She started laughing and giggling. "Father running in the Comrades," she said. "Oh, what a thought!" The next morning, I met her at the entrance to the OMI Provincial House. She had to open the locked gate for me. With her wonderful laugh, she let me in and said, "You will be our angel." As I tripped going through the door, I said, "A stumbling angel!" The OMI Provincial said the Mass, and the chaplain at the university assisted. The chaplain invited me to come to the noon Mass at the university the next day. I did and it was "just you and me, kid." He and I were the only ones there. I hope he does not get discouraged. He just came back as chaplain after several years of absence.

Volunteering

A month ago, I started volunteering at Mkuhla House on Thursday mornings. A van driver picks up the children from King Edward Hospital at 9:15 a.m. The drive to Mkuhla House is only about a mile. All the children are being treated for cancer. The idea is to let them leave the hospital for a few hours and enjoy some time at play. Usually, we have between ten and twenty kids. They are all under nine and most of them are under five. Generally, they cannot speak English.

Sometimes we visit and play with the children at King Edward Hospital, as well. Linda, who can speak English, is a Zulu child. Her father is a principal of a school. Linda is six years old. When I learned she was being released from the hospital and returning home, I went to see her. Linda had become very attached to me. We would put puzzles together or bat balloons with a badminton racket. This day, she told me to close my eyes, and then she led me to her room. We had to look through the keyhole because the room was locked. Linda asked me to pick her up. She wrapped her legs around my waist. Then she said, "Hold me real tight." As I gripped my arms around her, she bent backward and tried to touch the floor with her head. I told her she was very pretty, very bright, and I wanted her to study very hard. I kissed her and said, "I love you." Her mother came over and there were tears in her eyes. Some of the attendants at the hospital and Mkuhla House do not seem to interact much with the children. Perhaps they are very busy or do not want to face the pain of loss again and again. Most of the children do not live long. To me, you have to give your heart away, whether it hurts or not. "We are born to love, we live to love, and we will die to love still more." I like that quote of St. Joseph Cafasso, an Italian priest who died in 1860.

This morning I auditioned at Tapes for the Blind. Durban is the main center where these tapes are produced in South Africa. The woman in charge said, "I love your accent." They are anxious to use me for recording American books. The director said I had a good strong voice and she would like me to start with John Grisham's *The Client*. Supposedly, they match the voice with the book. I had asked about reading children's books, but I guess they do not focus on that. So, *The Client* it is.

The other area of volunteering that I thought about is working with AIDS patients. Sometime this week, I will talk to someone about it. Between volunteering, my commitments to the university, and my Zulu classes that are coming up, I will be busy. However, I feel very strongly that I have to be working in the community and not just at the university. I could not keep my inner balance if I did not do this. Of course, I know a lot of people probably think I lost my balance a long time ago—the word unbalanced quickly comes to mind!

In the News

A Japanese team made it to the top of Mount Everest but, in the process, they left some distressed Indian climbers to die on the slopes. There was a similar story with a South African team that left their photographer behind, who died. Supposedly, the survivors had been "overcome by summit fever." One of the Japanese climbers said in the news, "Above 8000 meters is not a place where people can afford morality." That is a chilling quote! A Norwegian expedition leader summed it up. "Friendship, closeness to nature, building up a relationship with the mountain has gone. Now it is an attack and climbers have to reach the summit at any price. People are even willing to walk over dead bodies to get to the top. This is my second visit to Everest and I shall never come back."

Also in the news was the loss in Cape Town of African National Congress candidates to National Party candidates. Ironically, the spokesman for the National Party (formerly the party of apartheid) was a black South African. "They need to take the loss like a man." he said. "Cowboys don't cry." Has he been watching too many John Wayne movies or what?

Finally, I cut this out of the Sunday paper: "Scientists examining the relics of a Seventeenth-Century saint venerated in the central English city of Birmingham have discovered that his casket contains three legs." That is a front-running candidate for the title of Saint of Transplants. If you are ever in a three-legged race, he is the man to pray to!

Mkuhla House—June 20

Today I was at Mkuhla House. Thursday mornings I play there with the children. Mkuhla House is also an outreach center where some adult cancer patients stay while they are receiving treatment. However, I have never met any of the adults. One of the large rooms is used as a play center for the kids. All the donated toys are locked in cupboards until the kids arrive. There are usually two to four volunteers there on Thursday.

I always let the kids just grab the toys they want to play with. Maybe it is a tricycle, a doll in a carriage, or a model car. After a while, I take out something myself. It might be tennis rackets and balloons or a board game like Mouse Trap. Within minutes, there are kids around me wanting to play. Today four or five boys circled me. We were putting together Lego bricks and making a zoo with little animal models. Another volunteer came up to me with this crying two-year-old child. The volunteer was not sure if the child was a boy or girl. Sometimes it is hard to tell. All the children are dressed in blue cotton pajamas that look about as drab as the old Mao uniforms. Plus, their heads are bald from the chemotherapy. Some wear pull-on caps. The volunteer said, "He just won't stop crying." I looked up from my pile of building blocks. The child just stretched an arm to my neck and climbed into my arms. He (or she) stopped crying right away. He put his head on my breast and his tiny arms partly around my ribs. Then, he just looked up at me. I held him for a long time. The nurse could not coax him away with cookies or juice. He just kept looking up into my face. I sang, "Yes, sir, that's my baby." Then he just closed his eyes and snuggled in deeper. Of course, he did not know what I was singing. Only one or two of the older children even speak English—and very little.

Someone asked me whether being around the children depressed me. Between this week and last, one of the children died. When you come, you never know who will be missing and without any explanation of what happened. Being with them does not depress me at all. I play with them and laugh with them. I just wish that the child's mother could have had those moments with her baby. These are children whose parents are in rural areas so they are left at the hospital for treatment. Some never see their parents again. In some cases, cancer just moves too aggressively; in others, the parents cannot afford to come back into the city. Of course, some of the families are just afraid of the disease and feel it could spread to other members of the family. That little child in my arms just wanted to be held. No doubt, some of the children become very jealous of your attention to the other children. You become their friend. When you try to coax another child into the game and coax yourself out, they just stop playing.

A hospice nurse in St. Louis once told me that I have a gift for working with people who are dying because I am not afraid of them. If so, I hope God never takes the gift away. There is something intense and holy about these brief relationships.

Safari in Kruger Park—June 22 to June 26

When I told Dave and Isabel, the owners of Rent-and-Drive, that I was going to Kruger Park, they gave me a free upgrade on a newer-model Nissan Sentra. It is a 1991 or 1992, and has power-steering, power windows, a tape deck, and automatic transmission. Dave said he did not want to get a phone call that my 1989 VW had broken down somewhere. He preferred that I take the newer car, which he had the mechanic check from top to bottom. I picked up the Nissan on Friday, June 21. I think Dave was almost as excited about the trip as I was. Dave kept saying to Isabel that maybe they should not be so concerned about money and business but should get out and see things. Both he and Isabel asked me to come to their home for a visit when I got back and even lent me one of their old tourist maps from Kruger.

It is an all-day drive to Kruger from Durban, so my first stop was Nelspruit, about 65 km outside the park. Nelspruit is in a valley called De Kaap, where some of the biggest gold discoveries have been made. There is some beautiful scenery on the way, including the Krokodilpoort Mountains. When I rolled into town, it was about 3:30 p.m., and a car rally was going on. Half the streets were blocked off with police tape, and I could not get to my hotel. One of the policemen lifted the tape so I could park and watch the rally.

While waiting for the next car to roar through, I talked with a young white couple that I met on the street corner. They were probably in their early twenties. Despite their young age, they were pessimistic about the changes in South Africa. They cautioned me about violence. I told them Nelspruit looked like a little country town where crimes would likely be misdemeanors at most. They seemed to see the town as much more threatening. When I saw all the crowds lining the street in Nelspruit, I thought Mandela was coming to town! I happened to mention the recent incident at the University of Natal where I was knocked to the ground while waiting to see Mandela give a speech. The young man immediately said, "See, now you know what we're up against here." Yes, the incident was scary, and I would be cautious about putting myself in another situation like that. However, I said that I did not attribute what happened to maliciousness on the part of the students, only unrestrained enthusiasm. They were determined to see Mandela up close. I wanted to see him too! Despite our different perspectives, this young guy was very gracious. He said that if he were not working, he would have enjoyed taking me around himself.

When the rally concluded and the police tapes were taken down, I finally drove to my hotel, The Paragon. There were only two large hotels in town to choose from. The other one, The Promenade, was filled. Both had a three-star rating, but, in the case of The Paragon, this was probably too generous. The desk clerk gave me a key to my room. Since there was no elevator, I hauled my luggage up the stairs and turned the key in the room lock. Soon as I opened the door, I saw clothes scattered on the bed and around the room. Someone had already checked in. This did not inspire confidence. I phoned the desk clerk from the room and waited in the hall. The hotel maid brought me another key. The room was small, and the bed was about three-quarters the size of a single. At rock-bottom prices, it was quite adequate. I barely had time to throw my suitcase on the bed before I headed out to Mass at St. Peter's Catholic Church.

After Mass, it was very dark and I was not sure I could find my way back to the hotel. When filing out of the church, I shook the priest's hand. "I think I'm lost," I said. "Do you think you could give me directions?" He replied, "I'll draw you a picture." As he spoke, I realized he thought I meant directions to heaven! "No," I interrupted. "Just directions to my hotel will do for now." Then, he told me to wait in the sacristy. He came back, and we started chatting. From his strong accent, I assumed he was Polish. His name was Joseph König. For two years, he took courses in spirituality at St. Louis University. Since I was born and grew up in St. Louis, he asked if I knew certain people. When he was at St. Louis University, he spent most of his time in Fusz Hall, where Jesuit scholastics lived. No one offered to take him around. That was unfortunate because he was such a nice guy. He insisted that he drive to my hotel and let me follow in my car so I would not get lost. When we arrived at the hotel, he jumped out of the car, chatted some more, and shook my hand. He was a kind man.

As soon as I returned to the hotel, I enjoyed a buffet in the hotel dining room and chatted with the chef. He said he had been preparing meals there for forty years. His name was Meshach and, yes, he had two brothers that his mother named Shadrach and Abednego. We laughed, and I told him he was a wonderful cook. His desserts were so sweet that one bite was enough to satisfy even a sweet tooth the size of Jumbo's tusk. I was the only customer in the dining room that late, so Meshach and I talked and laughed across the room.

That evening was very cold. There was no heat in the room. Since I only had one light blanket, I pulled it over my head like a tent and tried to keep warm from my breath. In the morning when I stepped out of my room, there was this terrible smell. Turning in the room key, I asked the desk clerk what it was. She said it was from the Mondi paper mill, but most of their guests just assumed the hotel sewers had stopped up.

Anyway, I was on the road to Kruger Park early Sunday morning. There are eight gates into Kruger. I entered the Malelane Gate in the south of the park and made my way to Skukuza and then to Satara where my accommodation was. On the way, I saw an elephant close-up. While I was watching it, a leopard tortoise, struggling across the road, decided to get out of the heat and traffic by seeking shelter under my car. His species is among the largest tortoises; some can weigh almost 120 pounds. I asked some tourists in a nearby car to direct my wheels around the tortoise and back on the road.

In Satara, I stayed in one of the tourist huts, which had two beds and a bathroom, all covered by a thatched roof. On the verandah was a refrigerator. Here were all the comforts of home. One of the park maids was sitting on my verandah wall when I pulled up; she was talking to another maid. As they saw me, they got up. I told them, "Don't move on my account." One of the maids had a dinner plate on her head; it held her supper. She looked so delightful that I asked if I could take her picture. Both maids asked me where I was from, and we talked for a while. At Kruger, with few exceptions, the guests are white and the employees are black. I am not sure why black South Africans generally do not come to the park. Is it too expensive and far away? Are they not interested in watching animals in a park? Do they anticipate being excluded? Are they fearful of standing out? I do not know, but I hope that changes.

I had dinner in the main building. It was a very good buffet. On a separate table were fresh salads, bread, and a huge glass bowl of vanilla ice cream. It reminded me of old movies or black-and-white snapshots of wealthy colonists in the bush with all the trappings of home. When I walked back to my hut, I was stunned by the vividness of the stars—bright points of light set in blackness. A cloud of galaxies just reached out!

The next day I drove to Letaba. On the way, there was plenty of game: impala, zebra, giraffe, warthogs, and wildebeest, among others. Plus, there were beautiful birds. My favorite was the lilac-breasted roller. In addition to lilac on its breast, it has feathers the color of turquoise and jade. At first, I did not want to take my eyes off of it, but the more I drove, the more I began to see these birds. At Letaba, there is a wonderful museum. It has about a dozen matched tusks along with photos and stories of the elephants to which they belonged. Each elephant has its name. When you stand by the tusks, you realize how big they are. You can even touch them. The museum also shows elephant fetuses at various stages. It is amazing to see these perfectly formed miniature elephants with a tiny trunk and tiny feet. One looked like a three-inch ivory carving. I learned too that, unlike humans, elephants have a brain at birth that is only one-quarter developed. They have this extraordinary growing capacity for learning and memory.

There was also a picture of a car that an elephant had smashed. Two tourists left their car to see a herd of female elephants and their calves. Not surprisingly, the male elephant got wind of them, was upset and protective of the herd, and demolished the car. He ran his tusks right through the steel door and after that stomped all over it. It looked like it had been through a car crusher at a scrap yard. Fortunately, the tourists were not in the car and escaped alive. I chatted for a while with the museum attendant and told him about my close call with an elephant at Hluhluwe. After seeing that car, I felt watched over.

For the next four days, I saw as much as I could of Kruger Park, taking the less-traveled dirt and gravel roads whenever possible. I left my cabin when the security gate opened at 6:30 a.m. and came back between 4 and 5 p.m., shortly before the gate was locked for the evening. One day I was going over a concrete bridge. There was no other car in sight. The bridge was covered with baboons. For some reason, I thought I could just creep along and the baboons would part like the Red Sea. Well, these baboons were smart enough to know that I am no Moses! The next sounds I heard were two thumps, then three. When I looked in my rear-view mirror, I saw alien fingers sliding down the back window—like E.T. in Steven Spielberg's movie! Next, I looked out my windshield and saw a baboon's face staring at me upside down. Suddenly the trio started playing bongo music on the roof of my car. Eventually, I drove the car over the bridge at about 1 mph, but the baboons just kept their seats. Finally, they jumped off and I could see their hand and footprints all over the hood of my car. It looked like handprints from Lascaux or Altamira!

At another time, I came across a huge elephant by the side of the road. Immediately I stopped the car. No one else was around. The elephant walked into the middle of the road and looked at me. He started walking to the car. By now I knew this meant "Back off!" Then another elephant came into the road. It was the most wonderful sight. These two giant beasts took their trunks and delicately felt around each other's heads, trunks, and bodies. It looked like an elephant embrace to my non-scientific eyes. As I drove through the park, even the clouds began to take on animal shapes. In no time at all, I saw elephants in the atmosphere as well as in the biosphere!

On the bridge overlooking the Olifant River, I got out of the car and looked around. It was like paradise. There was a family of elephants splashing in the water. On the rocks were some crocodiles sunning. At another spot were a group of hippos bobbing.

There is no way to describe all the sights. Once I passed a tree and a big baboon was sitting on top of it. He looked like a sentinel, and maybe he was a lookout for a nearby baboon troop. I watched zebras scratch their heads on the rump of the zebra beside them. Two giraffes twisted their necks, one around the other. The longer I was in the park, the more my other senses started kicking in. I did not just see the elephants; I heard them cracking the bark from trees. I heard the zebras rustling the tall grass as they slid through. While I started off looking for the big wildlife, as the days progressed I was even noticing the rhinoceros beetles on the ground.

Everyone wants to see a lion. At first, I went to Timbavati to see if there were any lions. Timbavati is known for its white lions. When I pulled in, I was the only tourist in the rest area. A black attendant walked up to my car. "I was looking for white lions, but you're not one of them," I joked. "In fact, with you walking about, I don't think any are around." He laughed charmingly. We started talking and he said he wanted to show me something in the bush. "Should we be walking in the bush?" I asked. "You don't have a gun or stick or anything." He swept his hands up to his face and said, "I have these." I took that to mean that he could smell a lion or hear a lion if one were around. His senses were more fine-tuned than mine. Then he showed me a sheer rock face and he wanted me to climb up for a better view. "I can't climb up there," I said with an astonished smile. "I'm not a mountain goat." He just kept saying, "Come. Come." As I began navigating the rock face, I kept insisting. "I can't do this," I whined. "I'm not like you, trim and fit." Again, he said, "Come. Come." Before I knew it, I was at the top of the rock. My legs and balance were a bit shaky on the slanted rock, but I was at the top. I told my insistent guide, "I think I could climb Mount Kilimanjaro with you to help me!" It is such a great feeling to do something you did not believe you could. As we were heading back, I asked his name. "Daniel," he said. "Daniel Mchauke." I laughed. "Daniel, you have the right name," I said. "You are brave like Daniel in the lion's den!" Daniel told me that the next time I came to Kruger, I should stay in the hut with him and his wife, and he would show me leopards at night. A leopard hunts from a tree near his house. Daniel also said he would help me with my Zulu even though he was a Shangana. I took pictures of him, his wife, and his little house, which I will send to him. Such unexpected grace!

When Daniel and I returned to the rest area, we sat and talked some more. I also talked with his wife and gave them both the food that I had in my car for my lunch. By that time, six white South Africans had come to the rest stop. They stared as I was talking and laughing with Daniel and his wife. Finally, an older woman, on her way to a trash barrel, came over to me and asked where I was from. When I told her, she asked if I liked South Africa. However, she never spoke to Daniel and his wife, and they never spoke to her.

Daniel told me a road to take where there had been some recent lion sightings. I went in that direction. On the way, a car stopped and the driver told me about a lion sighting 2 km ahead. When I came to the place, there were about three cars parked. I rolled down my window and asked one of the drivers what they were looking at. He pointed to a mound behind which you could just see three pairs of lion ears; each had a black spot with a touch of white inside. I started to edge my car alongside those that were parked. In trying to park, I accidentally set off the electronic burglar alarm in the car: woo-woo-woo. When the lions heard that, they sat up fast, and we all had a much better view. Unfortunately, in trying again to maneuver my car, I set off the alarm at least two more times. The mechanic at my car rental had put two separate alarms on the car. It was very confusing because I was never sure if both alarms were off. Each time the alarm went off, the confused lions suddenly looked up. Part of me thought the people should be grateful for the free show! Understandably, some just glared at me. They were probably saying, "Who is this nut?" Ah, Hamlet, that is the question! At another location, I glimpsed two mating lions. It was funny because a warthog unexpectedly ran right by them but they were not concerned about dining at that time. It was the warthog's lucky day.

On my last day in the park, I went out very early, hoping to see a leopard. Other cars with early morning tourists were passing me on the dirt road. They were rushing to see a leopard or lion when beauty was all around them. You could see zebras and giraffes that seemed to float through the white mist rising from the earth. There was a stunning sunrise that filled the whole sky with orange and rose.

My chances of seeing a leopard were very poor at any time, but especially during the day. As the day wore on and I had not seen a leopard, I said a prayer to my mother, who had died about ten years ago. It happened to be her birthday—June 26. She knew how crazy I was about animals and often told me so! With about an hour or so to go before I had to leave Kruger, I took a turn down a dirt road and drove slowly. Literally in a flash, an impala raced in front of my car followed by a spotted cat. I saw the cat take the impala by the throat and pull it down near a tree. When my breath came back into my body, I also saw a van parked a few yards further up the road. The driver, a woman, rolled down the window of the van and told me that a cheetah had killed an impala. Now the cheetah was supposedly lying behind a log. I looked and saw the log, but I did not see the cheetah. The woman invited me to come inside the van with her husband and daughter. That way, I could sit higher up and have a better view. With the cheetah supposedly about twenty or thirty feet away (and with a ground speed of 70 mph compared to my 3 mph, at best), I stepped out of my car and walked to the van.

The couple were very nice. Their daughter was about thirteen. I let her use my binoculars. We stared at the log for a long time. The man had read that a cheetah does not eat its kill right away, but waits about thirty minutes. "To let it get to room temperature," I quipped. Our wait was well rewarded. We saw the cheetah get up, walk around, take the impala by the throat, effortlessly lift it, then drag it to the spot where the cheetah would feed. I told the family about praying to my mother on her birthday so that I would see a leopard. Then I explained that my mother did not know her animals very well, so I suspect she thought one spotted animal was the same as another. "I'm going to consider this my gift, my leopard," I laughed. There was sad-and-sweet laughter from that family as well. Life is strange. I will never see any of them again, but for those few minutes, we shared a bond—and now share a memory. They are tucked away in a few of my brain cells and, in that sense, are a part of me.

As soon as I left Kruger, I felt differently. For four days, I had been immersed in all that beauty and wildlife. The tarmac and the buildings outside the park seemed sterile. Also, I had become so accustomed to driving at turtle speed, that I felt like I was doing low-altitude flying when I started back on the highway.

Hluhluwe—June 27 to July 1

When I left Kruger Park, I stayed overnight again in Nelspruit and departed for Durban at about 5:15 the next morning. At first, I could not find the highway. I pulled the car over to the side of the road and looked at a map. A man who was stopped at a red light rolled down his window. He asked, "Is there a problem?" When I told him what highway I was looking for, he said it was about thirty feet straight ahead. As I started driving, the fog was so bad that I could scarcely see the turns in the road. Because there are often people walking on the side of the roads, I had to be very careful.

Unexpectedly, a large cat-like creature ran in front of my car. It may have been a spotted genet. Of course, I was afraid that I might have hit it, so I turned my car around (a very dumb thing to do in the fog) and drove back down the highway. There was no sight of roadkill or injury. To see the sunrise and the fog lift was reassuring.

When I returned to Durban, I took the Nissan to the car rental agency, went to the flat, collected clothes for laundry, and drove to the laundromat. Later, I repacked for the trip to Hluhluwe the following day. This was a week to indulge in wildlife viewing.

Even though I have been to Hluhluwe several times, I always enjoy it. It is not as easy to spot wildlife there, but that makes the sightings even more exciting. This time I saw about fifteen rhinos, usually in pairs of two. Three of the sightings were very close-up. At Kruger, I had not seen any rhinos so this was a real treat.

I did not leave for Durban until 6 a.m. Monday, July 1. Then it was back to work by 10 a.m.

Archbishop Hurley—July 3

I received a phone call in the evening. It was Archbishop Hurley, calling to give me a lead on some AIDS efforts. He gave me the name of a man, Paddy Kearney, who headed an interdenominational committee called the Diaconia of Churches.[33] Archbishop Hurley suggested

---

[33] According to Greek scholars, Diaconia refers to ministry, service, support, or relief. It is found in the Gospel of Luke and the Acts of the Apostles. Diaconia can mean serving a meal, as well as the spiritual gift of serving others.

that I give him a call and see what they were doing. As we talked, I told him about my trip to Kruger and my excitement at seeing the cheetah kill. His reaction was, "Yes, but the poor impala." I admitted that I am very sentimental about animals, but I know it is the nature of cheetahs to hunt and kill. "That's how God made them," I said. The archbishop replied, "This is disturbing in itself." Right away, I let him know that I often think of that. This way of nature came from the mind of God. Sometimes it seems so cruel, even though we are projecting all our emotions and fears on an animal. Still, what does it all say about God? The archbishop said it bothers him too and he has a lot of questions to ask God. I told him, "Well, when you find out, let me know!" He said, "Yes, I probably will go before you!" He has a good sense of humor, and I enjoy talking with him. We also talked about Archbishop Desmond Tutu. Archbishop Hurley said he was a very good man. He related a story about someone who had been a staunch Anglican until Tutu was elected head of the Anglican Church in South Africa. The man said, "I was okay until the Anglicans put Tu and Tu together."

Consul General Party—July 4

I went to work in the morning. Then I had to wait for someone from the car rental agency to bring an oil cap. When I was returning from Mass early in the morning, I noticed smoke coming from under the hood of the car. I popped the hood and there was oil everywhere. Luckily, I spotted that the oil cap was missing. The engine could have blown if I had kept driving for any length of time. When I stopped for gas the day before, the attendant put in a pint of oil. Apparently, he left the oil cap off. Buba from the car rental place was late getting to the apartment, which meant I was late getting to the Fourth of July party at the Consul General's house in North Durban.

Pamela Bridgewater is the Consul General, but she leaves that post for the Bahamas in about a month. When I arrived at the party, it was already in progress. There were cars parked in every available space on the street, as well as on the next street down. The wealthy homeowners were probably not pleased. The party was by invitation only. Fortunately, I brought the invitation with me. I thought all the Fulbright people had been invited, but it appeared that I was the only one there. When I spotted Kathleen Bethel, she told me that she did not receive an invitation. Using ingenuity, she convinced the security guard, a black South African, to let her, a black American, through the gate. By the time I arrived, most of the speeches were over, except the thank you speech from the guest, a woman who was an American astronaut. I was not there for her introduction. There was Zulu singing by a group in traditional costume. Also, a black South African, whose first name was Raphael, sang *Impossible Dream*. He had a beautiful voice, but that did not keep people from chatting during his solo. There were no fireworks and no *Stars and Stripes Forever* (John Philip Sousa's march).

Even though it was a warm day, the guests were dressed in suits, ties, and heels—not like your typical American celebration. I was the only one who looked like I belonged in a backyard barbeque of middle-class America. This means I did not look like I belonged at a consulate party and would probably never mistakenly receive an invitation again! As I headed to the food line, I saw Archbishop Hurley. "What are you doing here?" I asked. "Well, I like a good party," he said. Then I recounted a story of when I was in New Zealand and threw a Fourth of July party for everyone at the data center. I made the mistake of asking the piano player at the beachside pub, who had British ancestors, to play *Yankee Doodle Dandy*. He asked what we were celebrating and I told him. "I'm not going to play that bloody song," he snarled. "We're the side that lost the war!" The archbishop laughed along with me.

There were hotdogs and hamburgers on the buffet, but I have given up meat. Actually, they did not look like American hotdogs and hamburgers. My celebration feast consisted of salad, cake, and Coca-Cola—eaten by the pool and the tennis courts to avoid the crowd.

Eventually, I ran into Kathleen again and we talked for a few minutes. Then I saw Deva, an assistant in the US Information Office. I asked him if I could see the Consul General's house. He showed Kathleen and me around. The downstairs area was filled with art and artifacts collected over many years in the US Foreign Service. The bedrooms were upstairs. The door to Pamela's bedroom had a deadbolt lock, and there was a surveillance TV pointed into the hall.

As I was leaving the party, some kids were collecting money in the street for the SPCA. I drove by, turned around, and then gave them something for their collection jar. They even had a sign: "Leave the money in our mailbox at the number provided." A much different approach to solicitation in this affluent neighborhood than in the city!

Tape Aids for the Blind —July 5

Today I went to my first recording session for Tape Aids for the Blind. I am reading John Grisham's *The Client*. The agency likes to match the voice with the book. First of all, they wanted an American accent. They think my voice has a boyish quality to it as well; the main characters in the story are eleven and eight-year-old boys. Readers record with headphones and a large microphone in a sealed room behind two doors. In two hours, I recorded twenty-nine pages. That may not sound like a lot, but my voice told me it was enough. I am monitored as I read. My monitor's name is Mabel. If I make a mistake or any noises originate from the recorder or from outside, Mabel backs up the tape and we do it over. Today the noise was from vacuums. Friday morning is office cleaning day. That always triggers a do-over. From the master tape, the agency produces cassettes. Supposedly, it will take me about four months to finish recording the book. Unlike the recorded books put out by the publishers, these are unabridged.

Margaret, the manager of the agency, gave me a tape of reader mistakes to listen to. Some were too dramatic (wailing and weeping with emotion), some snuffled, and some made the turning of pages sound like crackling thunder from an old radio show. One man with a "broadcasting voice" kept making mistakes. "Oh, Betty, we're not going to get anywhere today," he said on the tape. "Let's go to your flat and make love." They saved that piece of tape for posterity; hopefully, that does not include his wife. As their Number One reader, he recorded Nelson Mandela's *Long Walk to Freedom*. That had to be an enormous task, because the book, with over 600 pages, was almost as long as the walk! Margaret wants to introduce me to the head of Tape Aids for the Blind. I was told that she is a very dynamic and articulate woman. They would like to use me for other American books they have backlogged. We'll see if I do a satisfactory job on this first one.

At the Movies—July 6

Today, I went to see the *Feast of July* at the Musgrave Cinema. It was put out by Merchant Ivory and they always do quality films.

The African Macbeth—July 7

This afternoon I attended a production of *uMabatha* by the South African playwright, Welcome Msomi. It is an adaptation of Shakespeare's *Macbeth*. In 1969, Msomi wanted to write a play about the great African nations. Elizabeth Sneddon, who was then head of the Drama Department at the University of Natal, advised him to base it on one of the known epics. Msomi eventually chose *Macbeth* and wrote the play in a matter of weeks. The character of Macbeth was patterned on the Zulu king, Shaka, who killed his brother, Dingane. Lady Macbeth was Kamadonsela, Shaka's wife. According to the playhouse program, when the play was performed at the Aldwych Theatre in London, Peter Ustinov said, "It's the first time I've understood Macbeth!"

The production was at the downtown playhouse. The interior

of the playhouse in Durban is nice, but not African. When you are sitting in the theater seats, it is as though you are in a courtyard back in Tudor England. The walls of the playhouse look like Tudor buildings—brickwork, windows, and all.

The play was all in Zulu. Above the stage was a small computer display that told in ten words or less what was going on in the scene. The drama, costumes, dance, and drums were wonderful. I felt like jumping up on the stage, grabbing a spear, and hopping about myself. In one of the war scenes, there are Zulu warriors on the stage and others come running from behind the audience onto the stage. You almost feel like you are right in the middle of the battle, with Zulu warriors on all sides of you. At the matinee performance, the actors almost outnumbered the audience. There were 65 members in the cast. They seemed to give it all they had.

I was in the center seat in the fourth row. No one else was in the row except another woman about five seats away. At the intermission, I began talking to her. Pretty soon she moved and took the seat beside me. Her name was Agnes and she was an anesthesiologist at a local hospital. She was also Zulu. Agnes gave me a mini-Zulu lesson. She said the name of the play was *uMabatha* because it was talking about the person. If you were speaking directly to the person, the word would be Mabatha. Some people never speak to strangers. To me, Agnes was not a stranger, but a teacher and friend I just met

Snowmen in Africa—July 8 and 9

There were two meters of snow in the Eastern Cape. KwaZulu Natal was virtually cut off. The road to Johannesburg was closed. The media is calling it the worst weather for Southern Africa in human memory. Just to be prepared, I went to Woolworths and bought a few sweatshirts. Also, I made a trip to Hyperama at the Pavilion and bought a faux fur blanket. When I came back from shopping, one of the security guards was in the parking garage with Youngster, a German shepherd. Of course, I gave Youngster some dog biscuits that I have stockpiled in my flat.

Michael and Mtuzini— July 12

After 7 a.m. Mass at the OMI Provincial House, I went to Tape Aids for the Blind. Although I was scheduled for 8 a.m. to 10 a.m., the session was cut to one hour because Michael Berjak and I had to drive to Mtuzini. At Mtuzini, Ian Garland took us on a merry chase again. This time, it was two hours of climbing hills, sliding down hills, ducking under vines, and tripping over vines. It is very hard to gather systematic information from Ian. He is interested in trees, not data. Acquiring the data is my problem, of course, not his.

Musgrave Center—July 13

Saturday morning, I did some laundry. The day before, I had defrosted one of my refrigerators. As a result, I needed to mop up the water with my bath towels. That made it a good time to head to the laundromat. At the little shopping center nearby, there was a used book sale to benefit the SPCA. To support the cause, I bought one of Andrew Greeley's books and Robin Cook's *The Brain*, without any idea of what either novel was about. They simply carried the names of best-selling American authors. I ended up giving the books to Royal, my friend who works in the laundromat. She said she likes romances, so I am not sure *The Brain* will be to her liking; maybe Fr. Greeley's tale will. He is the Jackie Collins of the Roman collar set!

With my car packed with wet laundry, I scooted off to Musgrave Center. After trying on about a dozen pairs of sneakers in two separate stores, I finally found a pair that seemed to fit okay. Sizes are different here than in the States, so the only way to be sure is to try them on. Neither store had a Brannock device to measure my feet—those are the things that look like they belong in the hands of a medieval astrologer. In the second store, I found a pair of green suede Nikes. Well, if blue suede shoes were good enough for Elvis, green suede shoes are good enough for me. After looking down at the awful condition of my once-white sneakers, I was determined to go for a darker color. My choices were green suede, green suede, and green suede. The shoes cost about 369 Rand or $85-$90 US.

At Pic-N-Pay, on the lowest level of the shopping center, I picked up a few things. This is one of the largest grocery chains in South Africa and is one of the most modern. It is like a Schnuck's Super Center and has other things besides groceries, for example, dishes and school notebooks. It also has a section with imported (meaning more expensive) food items. Some of the brands are the same as in the US, like Kellogg's Corn Flakes, Bathroom Duck, Royal Pudding, Ajax Dish Liquid, Del Monte Fruit Cocktail, Hellmann's Mayonnaise—and, of course, Coca-Cola. Most of the brands are local, so it is Koos Peas instead of Green Giant. The check-out counters use bar-code readers just like in the US and you can pay for your groceries with one swipe of your MasterCard. Since I have lived in South Africa, I charge everything possible, and this is from a person who would never use a credit card in the US. Back then, I only had a credit card so that I could rent a car. However, when you are living in South Africa with fluctuating exchange rates, a credit card is the best way to go. You want to bring as little cash into the country as possible. At this point, I could be a consultant to Americans moving to South Africa!

Umhlanga —July 14

At about 9 a.m. this Sunday, I headed for Umhlanga. Along the way, I bought a Sunday paper from someone selling them in the street near downtown Durban. The paper was 3.60 Rand, which is about 90 US cents. When I got to Umhlanga, I window-shopped a bit. Stores do not open until about 10:30 a.m. The CNA was open, though. That is a book and stationery store. After browsing around, I ended up buying some chocolate bars for the two guards at the university security gate, who had to work from 6 a.m. to 6 p.m. this Sunday. I also bought Desmond Tutu's *An African Prayer Book*.[34] It has wonderful prayers. Some are from African saints like Augustine; others are from African traditions. Tutu said that one Zulu word for God is unkulunkulu—"the big, big one." Here, in part, are praises to unkulunkulu:

> All you big things bless the Lord.
> Mount Kilimanjaro and Lake Victoria,
> The Rift Valley and the Serengeti Plain,
> Fat baobabs and shady mango trees.
> . . .
> All you tiny things bless the Lord.
> Busy black ants and hopping fleas,
> Wriggling tadpoles and mosquito larvae,
> Flying locusts and water drops.

I am going to send this to my Jesuit pal in Ireland, Kevin O'Higgins. He made fun of me once for praying for the animals and the flowers. Looks like I fit right in with the African tradition![35]

When I left the store, I took the book and sat on some concrete steps that went down to Umhlanga Beach. On both sides of me were dark green bushes. In front of me were honey-colored sand and the Indian Ocean. Some men were fishing in the surf. A young couple was walking along the beach. I sat and read many of the prayers from the book. It was my own quiet Sunday service. A large black and white dog came up to me as I was sitting and sniffed the side of my

---

[34] *An African Prayer Book*, Doubleday Religious Publishing Group, T.H.E., 1995.

[35] Kevin taught philosophy in Asunción, Paraguay. We met when he came to St. Louis for further studies. He was pursuing a Ph.D. at St. Louis University and I was doing the same at Washington University. Sometimes our Missouri adventures included John Leonard, another Dublin Jesuit and good friend. John died 8 November 2006. Kevin's work in Dublin now centers on JUST (Jesuit University Support and Training) in Ballymun.

face. Then he went down to the beach. Shortly after that, an elderly woman came with a dog leash hanging around her neck. She said, "That dog is lost." Then she and her granddaughter went down to the beach to get the dog. At first, the dog hesitated, but then it came to them. The woman clipped on the leash and read the dog tag. They all came back to the steps where I was sitting. The woman said, "The dog is registered at the vet." I told her it was very kind of her and her granddaughter to look for the dog's owner. Of course, I never suspected the dog was lost. To me, he was just out cruising.

Later, three park guards came down the steps. I said, "Good morning." They turned around and replied, "Yebo. Sawubona. Kunjani." I laughed and said, "I'm from the United States and I only speak English." So, the one guard gave me a little Zulu lesson.[36] He said, "When we say, Sawubona, you say, Yebo. Ninjani." I told him I heard something like that on a TV commercial, "Yebo gogo." The guards laughed. That means "Hello, grandma." These guards were not elderly or female.

Two of the guards started down the beach and the other stayed to talk. He told me the beach was very safe and so was the one further north. "Stay where people are, though," he advised. We talked about how I liked South Africa. Then he told me his name was Innocent. I said, "Wow, there was a pope named Innocent." I gave him my name and extended my hand. Some people wonder how I can be happy in South Africa where I have no family and no longstanding friends. It is because I see the world in terms of these short, warm connections. It does not matter that they come out of nowhere and pass in minutes or seconds. The connection has been made. A whole life is made up of these connections for someone like me who is single and has been

---

[36] The Zulu greeting, "sawubona," means more than just "hello." It means "I see you." If you do not see someone with your eyes and your heart, you will pass them by, ignore their presence, push them away, and consider them less than yourself. For black South Africans, this is what apartheid did. In every country, there are those whose common humanity is not seen.

on the move for a great part of my life. The only unbroken connection is God.

After leaving the beach, I went to one of the shops in Umhlanga that sells carvings and masks. Usually, I stop there when I come to the beach and talk to the owner. This morning she had a small green-and-red parrot named Baby Shoes. The parrot was twelve years old, and its owner, a man, had died of cancer. In the last three months before his death, the man did not talk to his parrot. During that time, the parrot had plucked out a lot of the feathers from around its neck and on its belly. "This was because the bird was under stress," the store owner said. Still, this sad-looking parrot would talk. "Beautiful baby," the parrot said. "We walk by faith." There is a passage in the New Testament about Christ entering Jerusalem and the crowds cheering. Someone asks Jesus to keep his disciples quiet. Jesus says that if they remained silent, the very stones would praise God. Well, this Sunday, it was the very parrot! I have always been fascinated by how parrots, of all the animals, can imitate the human voice even though they do not have vocal cords as we do. What they do have, according to some scientists, is a unique brain with vocal learning centers.

When I left the shop, it was heading toward noon, so I bought a small vegetarian pizza for lunch—a Reggae—and some chocolate bars. At the outside café, I ate two or three slices of pizza. When I got back to the university, I gave two of the guards the chocolate bars. The third one, who I did not expect to be there, I gave the other half of my pizza. Every once in a while, I bring some treats for the guards on duty, like donuts on Sunday when I go to get the newspaper. All of them know me, smile, and talk when I drive through the gate. Sometimes, when they are complaining about being cold or tired, I will listen and say, "Oh, poor baby, poor baby." Then, we will laugh together. The other day it was raining. As I was coming through the gate, I held out my badge and told the guard not to step out of the hut and get wet. The other guard said, "You're always thinking about us." I am glad they feel that way because I enjoy each one of them.

The afternoon I spent reading a murder mystery, *The Potter's Field* by Ellis Peters, and working on my receipt ledger (for the IRS). The latter is one of my least favorite tasks.

Filming at Mtuzini— July 17

This week I talked to Jasper Cecil in the university Audio-Visual Department. Toward the end of this month, I will be taking a camera person up to Mtuzini to begin filming Ian Garland. Little did I ever think I would get involved in managing a filming project. For me, one of the good things about working in Africa is that I am doing things I normally would not do, like tramping through the bush, planning film sessions, interviewing people like Ian and Jobe, and designing a multimedia database. You take on tasks that you feel unprepared for, but you do them because you are the only one around and others have confidence in you. You develop this "of course, I can do it" attitude, stretch yourself, and start teaching yourself. In the States, the job would be turned over to a film company, a multimedia expert, and all the other experts. Here you have to be the expert or become one if you are not one already. I know that if I went to Pat Berjak and said, "Pat, you could find someone more experienced to do this—and in less time," she would say, "Nonsense, you can do it." Pat tells me, "You belong in Africa!"

No one could have been more supportive than Pat was of me. She had a tough time when she earned her Ph.D. years ago. Initially, she applied for a job in the biology department at the University of Natal but was not hired. Pat said that a less experienced man was given the job because the chairman of the department would not hire a woman unless there were no male candidates available. Being a strong woman, Pat decided to go overseas and become even better qualified. Today, I am told, she is highly regarded in South Africa and long ago passed by the fellow who got that job she wanted. Next year, Pat has been invited to China to present a research paper on seeds. Moreover, I have seen her with her students and she genuinely tries to bring them along; it is all about encouragement.

On a much different subject, today I talked with one of the guards in the parking lot of the Shepstone Building. I brought some dog biscuits for his guard dog, Lion. This Lion was more like a lamb. He let me pet him and ate from my open hand. I asked about Cyprian and Rea. The guard said Rea was sick. I have not seen Cyprian in a long time and have no way of reaching him. I wanted so much to buy Rea for him, so she would be out of the conditions at the kennel that Cyprian described. Now, I am afraid that one of these days, I will hear that Rea died just like Smokey. Monday, I saw one of the other German shepherds, Youngster. Right away, I went into my flat and brought some dog biscuits for Youngster. For the guard, I had some cookies. I wish I could go to the SPCA and adopt a dog myself. It is probably better, though, that I just "adopt" the guard dogs and the monkeys on campus.

King Edward's Hospital—July 18

Rose and I went to pick up the children at King Edward's Hospital. We were told that they were going to a birthday party for Mandela in Pietermaritzburg. When we arrived at the hospital, the nurses knew nothing about it. So, we packed the kids in our two cars. We had to carry some of them to the cars. They had no shoes, and their cotton pajamas were no protection against the very cold day. At Mkuhla House we took out some sweaters that had been donated and sized up each sweater with a child. Rose said, "When these children come back next week, they won't have these sweaters." I asked why and Rose said that the nurses take them for their children. The perception is that the children are dying and do not need them. If they do, someone will donate more.

Umhlanga—July 21

Sunday morning, I drove up to Umhlanga. At first, I thought I would head to Star of the Sea for 10:30 a.m. Mass. Fr. Carrington, the pastor, invited me to stop by some time. He said it was a beautiful little church that stood on a hill and faced the ocean. Fr. Carrington is 88 years old. He has white hair and a white beard. Plus, he still wears the OMI cassock—white with a black sash and dangling rosary beads. Certainly, he must be one of the last order priests to stay in uniform. On Saturdays, he has the 5:30 p.m. Mass in North Durban. Then on Sundays, he goes to the beach area, Umhlanga, and says a 7:00 a.m. Mass. After that, it is back to North Durban for a 10:30 a.m. Mass. In the evening, he heads back to Umhlanga for a 5:30 p.m. Mass. That has to be tiring for a man his age. Surprisingly, he told me that he does not want to retire. Father Carrington sees enough of retirement when he visits priest colleagues in the nursing home. For his part, he wants "to die with his boots on," or in his case, die with his cassock on! In his church, he only uses men as Eucharistic ministers, and they wear cassocks and surplices. While I think differently on that score, I understand him and I enjoy him.

Anyway, there was no 10:30 a.m. Mass at Umhlanga. I went to the beach and walked along the cinnamon-colored sand for a while. Stuck in the sand were a lot of tall fishing poles. I spoke to one of the fishermen, an Indian man who was there with his two sons. He had caught a small fish. Most recreational fishermen would have thrown it back. In my mind, this man was fishing for food, not for recreation. He told me that at high tide there would be 200 or 300 fishermen on the beach.

Eventually, I walked to a bench on the boardwalk. It felt like it was falling. You could sway it from side to side. In front of me were some spiny long-leafed plants. Maybe they were succulents or a kind of cactus. The only way to know would be to look them up in a plant book. The plants were about two feet high. People had carved their names in the leaves just as though they were trees. On the beach, an Indian woman was walking in a long black dress with a floral print. Out in the distance were about a dozen large ships, just fading against the horizon. To the south was the cityscape of Durban. I enjoy coming to this beach and looking out at the waves. You can see the sand caught up in them as they roll toward the beach. When the waves break apart, they have that same cinnamon color as the sand.

After I left the beach, I drove down Lagoon Drive to the Umhlanga Nature Reserve. I did not even know of its existence, so I thought I had better check it out. The sign has a rhino on it. Tourists might think they are going to see a rhino galloping over a dune. Instead, the rhino is the symbol for the KwaZulu Natal Parks Board. Every park sign in KwaZulu Natal has a rhino on it. The Umhlanga Nature Reserve has no hotels, businesses, or homes. There are just trees, plants, and dunes leading down to the beach. Some of the wooden-plank bridges that cross patches of the swamp have a real spring to them. I thought of an ad that runs here on TV. A car is going across a high suspension bridge and, as it is moving along, the planks of the bridge are falling into the water. It is "the car that outran the bridge," as the ad says. When the reserve bridges sprang back at me, I thought, "Will Doris outrun the bridge?"

Climbing over the dunes was a workout. I am always surprised when I succeed at a strenuous task. That is proof that anybody can do it. I may have a chunky body, but I am happy with it—and tell God so! It rarely gets sick, it has no lasting aches and pains, and it works just fine. Like a little tank, my body is not fast, but relentless in its progress. I remember this funny picture with a big fat cat that said, "I'm built for comfort, not for speed." As time goes on, I have become more conscious of thanking God for everything. When I hear the clock across the room ticking as I try to fall asleep, I thank God for my excellent hearing. The hard part is learning how to thank God when something goes wrong or what we perceive as wrong. Not just thanking God because He will get you through it or around it or beyond it; just thanking God at all times.

I remember hearing a story about an old Chinese man and his son. They had lost all their animals, all their wealth, and were the poorest people in the village. Everyone said, "Oh, such bad luck." Only a wise woman said, "How do you know it is bad luck?" Then one day some wild horses came racing down a hill and into an empty corral on the old man's land. He and his son quickly closed the gate. All of a sudden, they were wealthier than they had ever been before since horses were highly prized. Everyone said, "Oh, what good luck." A wise woman said, "How do you know it is good luck?" Then a warlord was coming to the village. He seized all the old man's horses for the upcoming battle and took his son as a soldier. The old man was worse off than he ever had been before. Everyone said, "Oh, what bad luck." Again, a wise woman said, "How do you know it is bad luck?" While trying to mount one of the wild horses for battle, the son was thrown off and crippled. Consequently, he did not go into battle. Later the old man and his son learned that the battle had been lost and all the warlord's men killed. His son, though, was spared death because of his injury. Everyone said, "Oh what good luck." Except for a wise woman who said, "How do you know it is good luck?" The story could go on and on while the message would remain the same. What looks like good luck may bring sorrow. What looks like bad luck may bring joy. Most of us become snared in our planning instead of finding grace in the moment. I like the saints who had a sense of humor. Their joy is freedom and humility.

OMI Provincial—July 26

I talked to Barry Woods after the seven a.m. Mass. He is the OMI Provincial. It was the feast of St. Ann and I told him that I prayed for Clem Burghoff, a priest-friend who practiced devotion to her. As pastor of St. Ann Shrine in St. Louis, Clem fostered that devotion in others too. That is how Barry found out I was from St. Louis. He told me that in 1973 and 1974, he was at St. Louis University doing a course in spirituality. Then he threw out a few names, like Dave Fleming, a Jesuit whom I had met. Barry stayed at Fusz Hall, where the Jesuit scholastics lived. Also, I learned that Our Lady of the Snows in Belleville was an OMI shrine. As often as I have been there to see the lights at Christmas, I never knew that.

Quiet Saturday Afternoon—July 27

On Saturday I did some grocery shopping at La Lucia Mall. In the afternoon, I watched a movie on TV: *The Candidate* starring Robert Redford. It is about the making and selling of presidential candidates. I have heard very little about the 1996 presidential campaign in the US. All of the sound bites come from CNN. Bob Dole already looks beat. Someone said he misplaced his campaign and is looking around for it. I need to go down to the US Consulate soon and register to vote absentee.

The Rock—July 28

I went to Umhlanga Rocks in the morning. Later I took Alan Amory and his mate, Richard, to see *The Rock* at the Musgrave Cinema. The movie is about breaking into Alcatraz to prevent a group from launching chemical weapons on San Francisco. Alan works in the biology department and Richard works as a statistician at the university. They are a gay couple. Several months ago, they invited me to their home for dinner. This was a way to reciprocate their hospitality. We went to dinner at Circus Circus in the Musgrave Center. Alan and Richard are both good people, and I enjoyed their company.

Zulu Class—July 29

Zulu classes started. They were supposed to be given in the building where my flat is—Shepstone. At the last minute, they were moved to the Memorial Tower Building. That is just a ten-minute walk from my flat. The classes are on Monday and Wednesday, either from 5:40 p.m. to 6:40 p.m. or 6:50 p.m. to 7:50 p.m. The earlier class has about forty people and the later one has about ten. The scheduler put me in the later class, but I am going to float between one and the other depending on my schedule. A man by the name of Jeff Thomas is giving the classes. I think he started his formal training in Zulu twenty years ago as a university student. He told us we need to find a mentor whose first language is Zulu. Then we can begin practicing with them. That is no problem for me. I can ask Pat, who delivers the mail; Clementine, who cleans the offices in the biology department; Herbert, Thiambi, and Mjabu who are in my department; Royal and Stella who work at the laundromat; and lots of other people that I come in contact with every day. I tried out my phrases on Clementine, Herbert, and Mjabu. They all seemed happy to help. I also could watch the news in Zulu on TV to learn some of the sounds and words.

Baloo—July 30

I almost adopted a dog, a white Maltese poodle that is four years old. His picture was in the Sunday paper on July 21. "Someone must be willing to take this dog," it said. "His time has run out." I did not see the ad until the following Sunday, July 28, when I was throwing out old papers. The next day, I called the SPCA. Very excited, I asked about the Maltese Falcon instead of the Maltese poodle! The SPCA said that they had Baloo since April 9th. This was the second ad they ran for him in the newspaper. In the first ad, they called him Sam. Now his time was up. Right away, I gave them my name and number and told them if nobody came to adopt the dog, I would. That night I dreamed my two dogs, Shiloh and Annie Bananie, who died several years ago, came back as spirits and started jumping on my bed—like dog angels! There is no need to puzzle where that dream came from. Today the SPCA called and said a family with a dog adopted Baloo. Some man even called the SPCA and offered 20,000 Rand for Baloo's upkeep, so he would not be euthanized. When someone puts a name and a face (even a dog's face) with a story about impending death, we humans usually rally around. The rest of the time, we keep from thinking about it. That is the sad part. When I return to St. Louis, I think I will go to the Humane Society to adopt a dog. Or maybe I should let my cats get reacquainted with me first.

Demo of Database—August 1

There is a steering committee that funds research at the biology departments of universities in KwaZulu-Natal. They came to University of Natal to discuss funding for next year. Present were about ten committee members and over thirty members from our biology department. The day was like a mini science fair. There was a full day of introductions and get-togethers, as well as time for committee members to look at posters and listen to presenters. Pat Berjak asked me to give a demo of the multimedia ethnobotanical database that I am designing. As a prototype, it is still in its early stages. Earlier in the week, Pat and Dehn, who runs the herbarium, gave me some photos. I scanned photos of Trichilia dracaena, a popular tree in Durban, as well as a picture of its seeds (very colorful in red and black) and its fruit. Finally, I imported these photos into the database using Microsoft Access 95. There was no time to scan video clips, but I intended to show how this could be done.

My demo was given in the Biology Museum. As I prepared for visitors, I was alone but surrounded by skeletons. There was an aardvark, whose last four vertebrae had broken off. The tip of his tail lay on the bottom of the display case, along with his lower jaw. Other specimens included a water mongoose; a bat-eared fox; a hedgehog and a mole with amazingly intricate and delicate skeletons; the skulls of a gorilla, chimpanzee, baboon, and man; a vervet monkey; a snake; and a porcupine. There were also taxidermy specimens, like the gray duiker, and lots of butterflies. While I was setting up the demo, one of the biologists walked into the room. She said it looked marvelous with me and the computer surrounded by all those specimens. I guess it did. They must have looked like a petrified audience—bored to death.

My demo was scheduled from 11:30 a.m. to 11:45 a.m. Presenters had ten minutes to talk but, for some reason, I had fifteen. The talks were running late so I did not get started until about 11:45, but I also did not need fifteen minutes. It was crowded in the little museum with all the people standing around. Afterward, they asked questions and I answered them.

Later I went to the luncheon that was set up in the seminar room; the finger foods were very good. There was plenty there for someone who does not eat meat—like me. That was the last I saw of the committee until 5 p.m. I was about to step into the third-floor elevator and head home. Pat Berjak walked out of the elevator with the committee members. As she passed by me, she whispered, "They loved your database." I was happy for Pat's sake because she has been so supportive of me. The next day, she told me that the committee wanted the biology department to find funding to keep me on and complete the project. That will be very difficult for them since the Rand continues to fall.

In the evening, I came back to the department to play Pictionary with about fifteen of the graduate students. We played in the break-room on the third floor. I stayed from about 6 p.m. to 8 p.m. The students were making crepes for dinner, but I had already eaten some frozen crepes from Woolworth's—not as good, I am sure. All that led to a discussion of pancakes in America. What is a pancake? What is a flapjack? What is a silver dollar pancake? How can Americans eat sweet pancakes for breakfast? In South Africa, pancakes tend to be small and strictly for dessert, for example, a four-inch pancake with ice cream on top. Yummy!

We finally got around to Pictionary at 6:30 p.m. There were four teams with four people per team. On our team, two of the people could barely speak English. One had to look up the game words in a Russian-English dictionary. It was a South African version of the game, so sometimes there were words like "Soweto." The evening was good fun. An all-South-African team won. Treating it all like the Olympics, I said our team won a Silver Medal, and another fellow on my team said "we played with honor." The winning team was very intense. Sometimes there were shouting matches between the two teams. I was glad my foreign presence did not keep them from being themselves and enjoying the game.

Taping The Client—August 2

Friday morning, I continued recording *The Client* at Tape Aids for the Blind. The session was from about 8:30 a.m. to 10:30 a.m. Initially, we wanted to begin at 8 a.m. However, the cleaners are working then, and there might be a faint sound of vacuuming in the recording booth. It does not seem to pick up on the tape, but we do not want to take any chances. I had to do a slight southern accent for Reggie Love, the woman lawyer in the story. I told Mabel, my monitor, that we should let the reviewers listen to it before I did any more of the dialogue in case it sounds ridiculous. However, she thought it was going "beautifully." So, we carried on. We are up to about 100 pages now. It requires a lot of concentration, not only to keep from making mistakes but to make the dialogue sound as realistic as possible. Recently, I came across the *Horse Whisperer*, a best-seller in the States now. I am going to check with Marilyn, the director of the organization, to see if they would like to record it. It is about a girl and her horse. Both are mutilated in a car accident, but both survive. The lady at the bookstore said it was a good book but very sad. One of the big Hollywood producers has already bought the movie rights, hoping for a hit like *The Bridges of Madison County.*

Zulu at the Laundromat

Later that same day, I repeated my few Zulu greetings to Royal at the laundromat. She was surprised and delighted. Immediately, she said something in Zulu to another woman standing nearby. Just from the tone of her voice and the context, I thought I understood. I said, "Royal, did you just say this person from America is learning Zulu, while people from here don't even try to learn it?" Royal laughed, "Yes!" Of course, she probably meant white South Africans. According to Royal, if you learn Zulu, you can also understand Xhosa. However, even Royal cannot understand the other South African languages, like Sesotho or Sepedi. When I left, I said, "Sala kahle" and she responded "Hamba kahle." This means "stay well" and "go well." The variation depends on whether the speaker and the one spoken to is staying or going. I know that, realistically, I will only pick up a few phrases but it is better than not trying at all.

Shopping and Gardens—August 3 and August 4

This Saturday I went shopping for books on multimedia at Musgrave and the Pavilion. Books here are very expensive. Even in the US, computer books are costly. The US prices on the ones I bought are $40 and $45. You cannot stay in the computer game, though, if you do not keep up with technology. If I am going to do this multimedia database for the department, I have to educate myself about multimedia tools and techniques. No one will send you to a class. You have to be your teacher.

Sunday morning, I went to the botanical garden for about an hour and fed the birds as well. All the while, I was singing that song from *Mary Poppins*—"Feed the birds, tuppence a bag." The garden is a beautiful spot. I know that in the computer field, there are all kinds of exciting things that are happening in computer animation and virtual reality. I could never become enamored of these. Certainly, I enjoy working with the computer, but it cannot hold my attention like nature does—or people. There was a program on TV today about the humpback whales in Hawaii. One of the women tourists said that looking into the eye of the humpback whale was like looking into the eye of God. Of course, it is! Just as looking into the computer screen is like looking into a mirror and seeing your image reflected. My interest in computers is rooted in my interest in people.

I left the gardens when it started to rain, just the gentlest of mists. Then I bought two mini-pizzas at the bakery and gave them to the guards on duty as I went through the security gate. The guards work twelve-hour shifts and stay in a tiny building that can accommodate about three people standing up. I know all of them now and bring treats when I have been off-campus. It is no big deal. I think some of them do not even have money for lunch.

Cold Season—August 5

Another cold! This must be the fourth or fifth one since I have been here. I only went to the office for a short time. While I was there, I called Microsoft to try and get the formula for estimating the sizes of video clips and scanned photos. We want to use both of these in our database, but video clips particularly consume huge amounts of memory. I do not want to embark on a design that we cannot afford. So far, Microsoft has not returned my call. At home, I did lots of reading, specifically in a book called *Digital Imaging*. I have stacks of homework in order to understand what our multimedia database will require. When I suggested to Pat Berjak that she look around for a multimedia expert, she said that she wants me to tackle this and learn something in the process. In the evening, I went to the Zulu class to pick up tonight's handouts, but I did not stick around. This cold and the twelve-hour cold tablet I took have made me too tired to concentrate on Zulu.

Open Wide—August 8

In the morning I went to Tape Aids to the Blind. They asked me to come in for a recording session on Thursday. Usually, my day is Friday. I also had an appointment at 10 a.m. with a dentist, Dr. Raikin. He was recommended by a couple of the professors in the biology department, including Pat Berjak. I just wanted him to check a loose crown. It spanned two teeth. Dr. Raikin did not want to mess with it; he said he might crack a tooth. Instead, he suggested that it probably would fall off during the holiday. "Just eat a toffee," he said. This was not encouraging news! At my request, he did make an effort. Applying only slight pressure from one of his instruments, the crown popped off. Then Dr. Raikin launched into an inquiry:

> *What do you call this? I've never seen anything like this. This isn't a dentistry problem, it's an engineering problem. I thought the dentists in the States knew what they were doing? We get all our tricks from them, but this is ridiculous. I don't even know what's holding this on. It's just a flat piece of gold.*

It was not flat but molded from my teeth. "Dr. Raikin, the crown has been in place for over twenty years, it's never come off, and you say there's no decay under it," I replied. "So how bad can it be?" There was a silent pause. "Right, I've just never seen anything like it," Dr. Raikin said. "You can tell Professor Berjak that this is a first for me." So, he cemented the crown, and I went away feeling I must have been going to a horse dentist all these years—a superb horse dentist!

National Women's Day—August 9

Today, Friday, is a national holiday, recognizing the contributions of women in the struggle for freedom.[37] Women now have political freedom in South Africa, but battering and abuse of women is an ongoing problem. Likewise, women have only made small headway in corporations, parliament, media production, professions, and other fields. From both viewpoints, a lot remains to be done, as is true of my own country, as well.

With the day off, I drove to Stanger to see the obelisk dedicated to Shaka (Tshaka), a famous Zulu king who lived from 1787 to 1828. He was murdered by his step-brother, Dingane, for the throne. From there I drove to Eshowe, the oldest town in Zululand. My ultimate destination was Nkandla Forest Reserve, 47 miles north of Eshowe. The tour book said it is still a refuge for wildlife, including leopards.

At Eshowe, I left the tar road behind and started on dirt and gravel. The landscape was like another "Thousand Hills," with one hill after another. The hills were winter brown and, for mile after mile, I passed nothing but rondavels, small houses, and people walking on the road. Some of the people carried long tools that looked like hoes; they were for cutting sugar cane. There were no stores, no gas stations, and no restrooms in sight. Eventually, I turned back because I was not sure if I was heading in the right direction. Roads are often not marked or not marked clearly.

---

[37] The history of this holiday goes back to 9 August 1956, when an estimated 20,000 women, primarily black but also from different races, marched to the office of the prime minister in Pretoria to protest the "pass" laws. The laws initially limited the movement of black males in South Africa. Those impacted had to carry pass books wherever they went. The laws were enacted to bolster apartheid and secure the white economy. In 1956, it was proposed to apply the laws to women as well. Four women led an historic march against this government plan: Lillian Ngovi, a black South African; Helen Joseph, born in England but settled in South Africa when she was 25; Rahima Moosa, born in South Africa and a member of the Indian community; and Sophia Williams, who at 18 was the youngest of the march leaders. The peaceful protesters sang a song that translated as "strike a woman, strike a rock." They were immovable.

When I returned to the university, I chatted, of course, with Sipho and Grace, two of the security guards. They are very nice and both are Zulu. I promised to take them to the beach sometime when they have a day off. Grace is a Roman Catholic. She has several children but is not married and does not want to be. Sipho, who is very handsome, is not married either. He and Grace are friends. Grace hopped in my car and I took her up the hill to the library. She told me that, when I go out, I must tell them where I am going and they will tell me if it is safe. Grace said many people would want to hurt me because I am white. We spoke about Amy Biehl,[38] a Fulbrighter who was killed about two years ago. She had been driving three black co-workers to their homes in a township outside of Cape Town.

The black South Africans that I speak with all the time at the university are very nice to me. They know that when I speak to them it is with an open heart, and we can talk about anything. I am not afraid to ask them questions, and I am not afraid to answer theirs. Today I ran into another security guard with a dog named Tiger. I picked up some biscuits from my flat and fed them to Tiger. My supply is getting low, so I have to stock up when I go to the store.

Saturday—August 10

Today I went out for the paper. At the bakery, I picked up a small quiche pie and pizza for the guards. I never know who will be on duty that day, but that works out better because then the treats are spread

---

[38] Amy Biehl was 26 years old when a mob pulled her from her car. She was murdered with machetes on 25 August 1993. Four men were convicted of her murder. Remarkably, the following year, Linda and Peter Biehl, her parents, founded the Amy Biehl Foundation Trust to discourage young people in South Africa from turning to violence. Two of the men who murdered Amy eventually worked for the Foundation. Then, in 1998, all four men were pardoned by the Truth and Reconciliation Committee headed by Archbishop Desmond Tutu. Amy's parents supported their release. In an extraordinary sign of reconciliation, they shook the hands of the men who murdered their daughter. Today, the organization in South Africa is simply called the Amy Foundation.

around evenly. I talk with all the guards as I come and go. Many know me by name and they all know me by sight.

Reluctantly, I did some cleaning. It was becoming chaos in the flat with all my papers and books spread about. With that chore behind me, I read for the afternoon. By 5:30 p.m., I was attending Mass at Assumption. In the evening, I watched a movie on TV—*Deceived* with Goldie Hawn.

Sunday—August 11

Today was Kathleen Bethel's last day in Durban. She is returning to the States. I drove her and Connie to Pietermaritzburg, the capital of KwaZulu Natal. Connie is the maid at the house where Kathleen has a flat. She speaks Zulu, so I practiced some of my Zulu greetings on her. Connie was so pleased. Kathleen wanted to see an art exhibit at the Tatham Gallery, one of the best in South Africa. Afterward, I treated Kathleen and Connie to lunch at the museum café. The food was good. Mine was spinach and feta quiche plus a salad. The exhibit, though, was not much to my tastes. Of course, it is always good to see artistic interpretations with different views of the world than our own. Some of the titles of the paintings were witty. One was called *Tiger and Tapestry*. It was a picture of a box of Tiger Oats in front of a tapestry drape. Another was called the *Sharing Mood of the Future*. This one showed a black rat and a white rat nibbling on a piece of cheese that was shaped like the map of South Africa. One of the black South African artists had some very disturbing pictures. *Pedophile* showed a human face made up of parts of babies and genitalia. *No Privacy in the Shack* showed a couple having sex at night while four of their children stared from their little bed. In *It Was Dad, Mum*, a young girl shows her mother her belly, swollen in pregnancy, while the horrified mother, with a black eye, gasps. The subjects are dark, but all the colors in these paintings are bright and bold.

After the exhibit, we walked around the corner to see the statue erected to Gandhi.[39] Then we went to the Pietermaritzburg train station, the site where Gandhi was evicted in 1893. Even though Gandhi had a first-class ticket, he was forced to leave the train because he was sitting in a first-class ("whites only") section. Supposedly, the station still stands just as it was in Gandhi's day. Although we searched, we could not find a plaque anywhere commemorating the historical event. The station, itself, was very old and drab.[40]

At the end of the day, I dropped Kathleen and Connie off at the Pavilion, where their car was parked; it was about 4:30 p.m. At 6 p.m., I watched a wonderful documentary on TV about Virunga National Park in Zaire. Now I want to go there! Virunga is a chain of eight volcanic mountains between Zaire and Rwanda. In addition to its beauty, Virunga has a strange animal cemetery. Its volcanic cones emit poisonous carbon dioxide gas. In the morning, it is like a mist. Any animal that ventures near the cones will die in seconds. The bones and new carcasses are scattered all over. As the day progresses, the gas lifts and it is relatively safe. Virunga also is a refuge for a colony of mountain gorillas and 30,000 hippos are in or near its river.

The photography of the gorillas was fascinating. It showed two of them watching intently as a lizard tried to make its way up a tree branch. The larger of the two gorillas would gently grab the lizard's tail and move it back a few inches. Then the lizard would make another start and the gorilla would bring it back to square one again. The gorillas were not looking at the lizard as food; they were fascinated by it. I wonder if we fascinate the gorillas as much as the lizard?

Since the documentary was made, a million refugees have streamed into Zaire, so I am not sure of the park's fate today. At times, saving the wild lands and animals of the earth seems hopeless. I know our

---

[39] The bronze statue was erected in 1993, exactly one century after Gandhi's death in 1893. Archbishop Desmond Tutu unveiled the statue on Church Street. Gandhi was 23 when he came to South Africa, and he lived there for 21 years.

[40] On 25 April 1997, Nelson Mandela presided over a ceremony at the Pietermaritzburg train station. A plaque records the incident of Gandhi being forced from the train. Later a museum honoring Gandhi was completed in the train station.

humanity demands compassion for human persons who are suffering. The earth and its wildlife demand our compassion too. Our theology and morality must include rainforests and mountain gorillas, humpback whales and snow leopards, golden lions and Monarch butterflies, and all of God's gifts in the natural world. I pray for the earth that we may not destroy all this beauty that God has given us in our greed and even in our suffering. It is our first home. How can I not love and pray for it? When the thought of all the human destruction becomes overwhelming, I live with the hope that God will somehow restore all nature's beauty. Nothing will be lost. Everything has its being in God, as we do. For me, there is something inconceivable about any life, once given, being destroyed forever. It remains to be seen what God thinks of all this!

Botanical Gardens—August 13

After Mass, I went to the botanical garden for an 8:30 a.m. meeting with Dr. Neil Crouch. He showed me some of the Precis databases. This is a national botanical database that has been under development since the 1960s. I need to see what Neil is doing and how it compares with what I am doing for the biology department.

At 7 p.m. I had a physics class in the Shepstone Building. Monday and Wednesday are Zulu classes and Tuesday is physics. The first physics class was on weapons of war. Toward the end of the class, when the two professors were talking about nuclear weapons, cruise missiles, and neutron bombs, they did a little editorializing about the Americans. "They won't take anything from you," one said. "Their policy is if you do something that's not in their interest, they'll bomb you right out of there."

At the end of the class, I walked down the steps of the theater to talk to the lecturers. I smiled and said, "That sounded like 'Yankee go home.'" They asked where I was from and what I thought about some of the weapon developments. They also asked if I had ever heard of the Manhattan Project. I said I had and reminded them about Oppenheimer who headed up that project. He said that excitement and momentum took over, preventing the scientists from raising questions of right and wrong. The design of the bomb was "so sweet," said Oppenheimer, you could not resist going for it. Then, after the first atomic test, Oppenheimer said "Now I have become Death." He explained that this quote was from Hindu scripture, Bhagavad-Gita. Oppenheimer felt that the physicists finally "knew sin." One of the professors spoke about the neutron bomb. It destroys people while leaving buildings and property intact. The neutrons go through steel but are stopped by water. Human beings are mainly water. Therefore, neutrons are destructive to human life. He said its development was hush-hush. I will ask my brother, the McDonnell Douglas engineer, what he knows about it!

Learning from Children—August 15

For the Feast of the Assumption, I went to 7 a.m. Mass at the Provincial House. Then I drove over to Mkuhla House. This is Thursday and the children come. They had to watch a video that showed a young cancer patient getting radiation treatment. All these tiny persons sat on the floor and watched the TV as intently as if it were *The Lion King*. The film showed a radiotherapist painting the marks on the young boy's body where the radiation beam would be directed. The whole treatment and post-treatment were shown.

Afterwards, I showed the children a book with Zulu words. I told one of the older boys (about eight) that I was trying to speak Zulu ("Ngiyafunda isiZulu.") and asked for his help. He could not understand English, but he knew what I was saying. I would point to a picture and the Zulu word, and then I would try to pronounce it. Zulu has about three different "clicks" that are part of the language. It is very difficult to pick up. When I pronounced a word, my young friend (because that is what he is), would laugh and laugh. He had this wonderful laugh! I laughed too. He would say the word again. I would try again, and again, and again. Sometimes he would pick up a toy animal or car, and then give me the Zulu word. I entered into this game by picking up other things and saying, "Yini lento?" What is this? I am convinced that the way to learn a language is to hang out with children! The Zulu social worker came over, and she started helping me too. She said she knows twelve African languages. Even a little Zulu boy about four years old said some words for me. It was lovely. I am going to see if they will let me be their pupil every week.

The boy who was helping me asked (through signs) if he could take his picture off the wall. We had about twenty photos on the wall from a party for the children. I recognized the word "auntie" in his request. Rose explained that he wanted the picture for his family. I told Rose that I am going to bring my camera next week and take pictures of the children that they can keep for their families.

We are supposed to take the kids to see the dolphins. I hope I can get some pictures with them and the dolphins in the background. Rose said, "They'll be over the moon." Rose is a terrific person. She brings two of her young children with her when she comes to Mkuhla House. Her little daughter is about one. Her four-year-old son, Brendan, has some mild brain damage. Sometimes, her teenage daughter helps out as well. Rose is just very giving. I think she is super. She also works with the Missionaries of Charity. Rose put a little ad in our parish bulletin to ask for volunteers since she was the only one going to Mkuhla House at the time. I called the number and that is how I got started. It was certainly lucky for me!

Zulu Rechristened—August 16

After I finished my recording session at Tape Aids for the Blind, I swung by Rent-and-Drive to take a picture of Dave and Isabel's new Rottweiler puppy. They told me his name was Zulu, but by the time I arrived with my Canon 35 mm in hand, they had renamed him, Joshua. The Zulu workers pleaded with Dave and Isabel not to name the dog Zulu. I told Isabel that makes sense because one of the meanings of Zulu is "heaven." I have been just as guilty of cultural insensitivity. I named my cat Kenya. When my Kenyan friend, a Jesuit named Otieno N'donga, heard this, he was really upset. "You can't name a cat Kenya," he said. "That's an honored name." Then he added, "You wouldn't name a cat Washington, would you?" I tried to explain that there were probably lots of cats and dogs in America named Washington, Jefferson, Reagan, Shakespeare, Socrates, you name it. This got me nowhere. I did not tell Isabel that Joshua, biblical scholars say, was the real name of Jesus. No wonder Jews do not say the name of God. Once you do, it gets tricky.

This afternoon I had a long chat with Joseph Kioko. He is from Kenya, as well, and was going back there for a month. I asked him to take a greeting card for some of my friends in Kenya. Joseph is such a gentle person and he has a great sense of humor. He is working on a Ph.D. in botany. Joseph is the oldest of nine children. His parents think he should get married instead of spending so long on his studies. In Zulu class yesterday, we learned that a man might be referred to as a boy until he was married. This is true in other cultures; you do not count unless you are married and produce children. Biologically, they are correct. Anyway, we talked about Joseph's village, where, he said, you can still suddenly come upon a lion, leopard, or cheetah. Joseph told me that a cheetah might come up to you on the road and rub its head on your leg like a house cat. You have to be very calm. Joseph admired the Masai who still hunt a lion in their passage from boy to man. I asked Joseph, "Do you ever wonder what the Masai think about?" He said, "They're just like us." Yes, except they kill lions with their hands and a spear! Also, they carry themselves with such dignity and presence. That could never be said of me.

Binti and Baby—August 17

I just saw on TV the news story about Binti, a female gorilla at the zoo in Brookfield, Illinois. A three-year-old boy fell into the gorilla compound and was injured. Binti, with her baby clinging to her, picked up the child and placed him near the door where the zoo guard could reach in and take him. Amazing! Maybe we would all be better off if this were *Planet of the Apes*.

The Dalai Lama—August 20

Yesterday I saw a notice on the Internet that the Dalai Lama was giving a talk at the University of Durban-Westville. The Dalai Lama, a Buddhist monk and spiritual leader of Tibet, is 61 years old. He became the Dalai Lama at the age of five and went into exile in India about 40 years ago. For many years, Chinese communists have been waging what the media call a war of genocide in an attempt to absorb Tibet into China. About 6000 Buddhist monasteries have been destroyed. In addition, there have been horrible crimes committed against the Tibetan people. Estimates are that a million Tibetans have been killed. The Dalai Lama received the Nobel Peace Prize in 1989 for his efforts to end the suffering in his country.

Immediately, I sent a fax requesting reserved seating, as the notice suggested. The talk was to be held at the Hindu Temple on the campus grounds. The university was originally an Indian university. Now, it is primarily a black South African university. There is an ongoing conflict between the black students and the administration and between the black community and the Indian community. The university has repeatedly closed down this year for demonstrations and strikes.

The talk was supposed to be at 5:30 p.m. Because I was unfamiliar with the route and the campus, I arrived at 4:30 p.m. Once on campus, I pulled the car over and asked a passing student for directions to the Hindu Temple. As it turned out, I was already close by. Luckily, I found an excellent parking spot in a lot across from the temple. Directly behind my parked car was a military vehicle filled with some guards. One of the black guards asked, "Are you with those Hindu people?" I told him I was there to hear the Dalai Lama speak. As I walked across the road, another guard motioned for me to come inside the temple. When I stepped inside, there was a third guard with a very large German shepherd. Security was high on the agenda. At the desk, I gave my name and showed my card for reserved seating. An Indian woman behind the desk started talking to me. She wanted to know where I was from and where I worked. When I told her, she wrote out a name and address for me. This would be a good contact for my work, she said. In turn, I gave her my name and phone number at the university.

Near the registration desk, there was a box, covered with decorative paper that had a slot cut into the top—like a homemade ballot box. The sign by it said that, if you had a question for "His Holiness," you should write it out and put it in the box. I did so. Then I walked down one of the aisles and found a seat in the temple. My seat was in row three, directly in front of the podium. The first two rows were for visiting dignitaries. That is a category to which I have never been assigned! Two of the ushers that were seating people in the reserved seats asked me to let others know that those seats were for the dignitaries who would be escorting the Dalai Lama into the temple—the mayor, the chancellor of the university, religious leaders, and others. They had name cards on the seats, like those at an invitation-only dinner.

Eventually, a couple sat in the two seats to my right and we started chatting. The man, who was next to me, mentioned that he was at the University of Natal and worked in the Music Department. He also was involved with the Jazz Center in the Shepstone Building. "Oh, I've been there," I said. "Someone told me that Dave Brubeck's[41]

---

[41] Dave Brubeck was a well-known jazz pianist and composer in America, who also played and recorded with the Dave Brubeck Quartet. Brubeck wrote the soundtrack for *This Is America, Charlie Brown*. That was an eight-part animated series with characters from the Charles M. Schultz comic strip *Peanuts*. The series aired from 1988 to 1989. At the time I met Darius, I had several albums by his father. Brubeck died in 2012 at age 91. Darius had a career as a jazz pianist, composer, and educator at the University of Natal, later named the University of KwaZulu-Natal. For fifteen years, he toured southern Africa with the Afro Cool Concept band. Also, he was a professor and Director at the Centre for Jazz and Popular Music at the university.

son was there, but I never met him." The man smiled. "That's me," he said. "I'm Darius." Very surprised, I said, "Wow, I've got some of your dad's albums!" Darius was from the United States. His wife, Katharine, was from South Africa. They met in New York. According to Katharine, during the first seventeen years of their marriage, they lived in New York. I looked at Darius and said, "So now it's your turn to do seventeen years in South Africa." He laughed, "That's right and I've already completed fourteen." We continued talking while we waited for the Dalai Lama. They were a very nice couple. An older Catholic nun came down the aisle. She started to sit in the second row. I told her, as I had been instructed, that the first two rows were reserved for dignitaries. "Well, that's not me," she said. "Me neither," I told her. I was glad, though, that one of the ushers pointed out a good seat for her just across the aisle. It was one of the dignitary seats, but it was not needed. So Sister became a dignitary by proxy!

The Dalai Lama finally came down the leftmost aisle, along with his entourage, at about 6 p.m. The host, Professor Leonard Saronsky, escorted him to a throne-like chair on stage. There were a few minutes while the hosts tried to pull their act together. I was just looking at the Dalai Lama and smiling. To me, it seemed he was looking right at me and smiling back. I laughed. He laughed and he never shifted his eyes away. I felt connected. After a while, I felt shy and lowered my head. When, in the next second or two, I look up, the Dalai Lama had looked away. Of course, maybe the Dalai Lama was near-sighted, staring at no one and lost in pleasant meditation!

At the beginning of the program, the UDW choir sang two songs. One was an African song and the other was *Love Walked In*. I watched the Dalai Lama move his right index finger to the rhythm of the music. When he finally spoke, it was in his native language. He had an interpreter who flew in from Oxford University. His features were delicate and he was slightly built. The interpreter relayed all the greetings to the hosts and the choir. Finally, the Dalai Lama said that he would speak in his "broken English." The interpreter was only there to supply occasional phrases.

The Dalai Lama spoke about tolerance for other religions. He saw other religions as a necessity since humanity came in so many temperaments and outlooks. For him Buddhism was good, but it was not something he would prescribe for everyone. Each person must make his or her own choice, including the choice not to belong to any religion or not to believe in God. He saw value in religion because it could help produce "good people." The Dalai Lama does not believe in a creator, but a "self-creator." He said he could accept a concept of God as infinite love or infinite truth, but not the personal God of Christianity.

The basis of his religion and his message was compassion. By this, he meant the recognition that we are all alike, and we all want to be happy. Therefore, we must respect each other and be concerned for each other. He talked about inner peace and that it could only be achieved through effort. It could not be bought in a store, he said, and it very rarely came from "above."

After his speech, which was not from a written text, he answered written questions. The first question was: "Do you think Gandhiji's philosophy of non-violence is applicable in South Africa today." He answered quickly and finally, "Yes." Then he looked to the interpreter for the next question. Everyone laughed at his brevity. The interpreter started to read the next question and I was surprised to hear it was mine. "Are you ever disheartened by the escalating destruction of the earth's beauty and wildlife? Do you have any encouraging words for the discouraging situation we face?" Well, it was a topic he liked because he spent the next ten minutes or more responding. He recognized the problem and said that when humanity was the source of a problem, it could be the source of the solution. The Dalai Lama thought the emergence of the Green political parties—the environmentalist movement—was an encouraging sign. He compared it to a political movement. If you fail, you try again. For me, the problem with that particular part of the answer is that once a species is gone, you cannot try again. Some failures are final.[42]

Another question asked what he thought about abortion. He answered that, as a Buddhist, he was opposed to violence and abortion was violence, killing. Then he qualified his answer because the increasing population of the world was threatening the life of the "whole" and so something had to be done. That something was family planning. He added that "we need more monks and nuns." This got a big laugh from the audience. It was interesting how he stood up for an unpopular position, without alienating anyone.

There was another question about his role as Dalai Lama. It was a long question that described his titles. Some say you are the reincarnation of this one, others say you are the reincarnation of that one, so how can all of it be true? He paused for a long time and looked a bit exasperated. "How do I explain this? As to my being the reincarnation of some higher being or God? No. Too much is made of that. I am the reincarnation of myself." The audience clapped. Then he spoke at length. "I only claim to be a simple Buddhist monk, and as long as I carry out the precepts, even Buddha cannot take this away from me. As far as being the Dalai Lama, tomorrow the people of Tibet could decide that I am not the Dalai Lama. Then, I am not the Dalai Lama! This is just a man-made title. I'm not concerned about it."[43] As he talked, I could not imagine Pope John Paul II coming out on the Vatican balcony one day and saying, "If tomorrow Catholics of the world say I'm not the pope then I'm not the pope." That would

---

[42] More recently, there are scientific efforts to save species from extinction, like the Frozen Ark Project. Researchers store cell tissue (DNA) of endangered animals. In 1994, the project started in England at the University of Nottingham. There are now 22 centers around the world.

[43] In 2013, the Dalai Lama saw changes in Buddhism as women took on equal roles with men. "I call myself a feminist," he said. "Isn't that what you call someone who fights for women's rights?" He also indicated that his next reincarnation could be as a woman. *Why is there no female Dalai Lama?* Michaela Haas, The Washington Post, 18 March 2018.

never happen. It is obvious why people find the Dalai Lama such a disarming person.

The evening finally ended at about 8 p.m. The Dalai Lama said that he gets up between 3:30 a.m. and 4:15 a.m., and by 8:30 p.m., his eyes are heavy. He exited by the far-right aisle, hugged the woman who directed the choir, and walked up the steps, hands folded, bowing, occasionally reaching out. It was a very enjoyable evening.

Food for Thought—August 21

Sister Gertrude was running down the street and I thought there was not going to be Mass this morning. She said, "Oh, no, we always have Mass." For a second, I paused. "But if I see Father running down the street," I said, "then I'll know there's no Mass, right?" She laughed and laughed. I get a kick out of the nuns. They often ask me to read at Mass, but they frequently give me the wrong reading. As I start reading the epistle, I can hear Barry turning pages and pages. Then when I read the psalm, there is total silence and Barry will say from the altar, "I have no idea where you are." When I go back to my place, I whisper to one of the nuns, "You got me in trouble again!"

Occasionally, I ask one of the nuns for a mini-lesson in Zulu. They are always happy to help. In Zulu class, Jeff Thomas, the instructor, happened to mention the importance of food in cementing relationships in the Zulu culture. Now I know why the security guards call me their friend because I regularly drop off something for them to eat. One of them, Sipho, gave me the Zulu handshake: shake, grab each other's hand with thumbs up, shake. He said, "That means I care about you, I love you, and you're everything to me." When I thought about food and relationships, I could almost hear Jesus saying, "Wake up, Doris! What did you think 'This is My Body' and 'This is My Blood' was all about?"

No Dolphins—August 22

We were supposed to take the children from Mkuhla House to Sea World today. When I got there, the outing was canceled. I think Rose and I were more disappointed than the children.

Yvonne, the assistant to the black nurse, was very concerned that we might be upset with her because the children were not allowed to go. While the children played, she asked us to sit encircling her. She explained that she was not a "boss" and it was not her fault. She even started to cry and seemed especially concerned that I understand. Later she asked me if I was going to stay in South Africa. "Please stay, forever and ever," she said.

Since I had brought my camera for Sea World, I decided to take pictures of the children. I brought each one outside by a little bird bath and trellis. That is where I took their pictures. In the end, I had a group photo. One of the smallest children, about two or three years old, just would not smile. Rose said he looked like a solemn little man. Who knows what he has had to go through in those short years? After all the photos were taken, I took one of the older boys outside and showed him how to take a picture. I told him to take one and next time I would bring it in to show him. Rose posed as the model. I did this because as soon as I came to the center today, he wanted to look at the camera that was around my neck.

I asked Rose to go with me next week to help pick out a bike for the older kids. The smaller kids have a variety of plastic tike bikes, but the older kids have nothing to ride. Sometimes you see an eight-year-old boy trying to ride a tricycle made for a three-year-old. It is like the opening clown act at the circus.

Short Film—August 23

I put in an hour of recording this morning at Tape Aids for the Blind. Then I picked up Mohammed Sheik from the university at 9:20 a.m.

He is a cameraman with audio-visual experience. I drove him to Silver Glen Nature Reserve to do some filming for the multimedia database. Julian Kruger, who works at the reserve, agreed to go on camera and talk about some plants. He had boyish good looks and did a great job. We were there for over two hours and only had about fifteen minutes of tape. I developed a real appreciation for professional film crews. One of the guys from the reserve came up to me and said, "You should get a job with SABC as a film producer." My response was, "Are you kidding?" Then I explained. "I don't know anything about producing a film," I said. "I'm just lucky Mohammed is here to tell me what it is I want!"

For the last shot, I asked Mohammed and Julian to use the coral tree. It turned out to be the best clip of all. While we were filming, two songbirds, a male and a female, flew into the tree and started feeding on the nectar. They stayed there long enough for Mohammed to re-aim his camera and get it on film. We will use it in the database, particularly in the section on animal interactions with plants. A vervet monkey also wandered out, but he was quicker than the cameraman and not at all interested in film stardom.

Colin and His Brooms—August 29

I went to the laundromat as usual on Thursday morning. As I was getting my laundry out of the "boot" of the car, Colin came up to me. He is a black South African who sells his brooms at the entrance to the shopping center. I bought two, which I do not need. When he approached me again, I spoke to him about his salesmanship. "Look, Colin, I want to be your friend," I said. "I don't want you to try and sell me a broom every time you see me." After that, it was fine.

Today he came to tell me that he had stored seven brooms at the shopping center overnight. When he came back the next day, someone had thrown them away. His English was very poor, so I was not sure

I understood him. I went into the laundromat and told Royal what I thought he had said. Then I asked her to speak with him in Zulu and find out what the problem was. She did so and confirmed that I had understood correctly.

Colin was afraid to talk to the manager of the shopping center, so I said I would. Royal called one of the security guards to come over, and he used his walkie-talkie to get in touch with the manager. Royal went inside the laundromat, and I waited for the manager. Eventually, a man in a wheelchair came toward me. I explained the problem. He was very angry and very bitter. I listened to him and then I said, "Well, now we've heard two sides of the story." He said, "There's only one side of the story." I told him that I was a regular customer of the shopping center. "I don't believe that," he said. "Well, why don't you ask Royal and Stella who work in the laundromat, or Danielle who works in the hair salon, or some of the clerks in the grocery store here or the film shop," I said. "They know me."

After that, he calmed down a bit. He wanted to know where I was from and what I was doing in South Africa. Yet, he was adamant that he did not want Colin on the shopping center lot "hawking" his brooms. I asked his name. Then I said, "Stan, things are so tough today that at least you have to respect someone who is trying to sell something instead of just putting out his hand or stealing your wallet." He told me that he would ask what happened to the brooms. Honestly, I do not know whether he will or not, but I extended my hand in goodwill. When he left, Colin came up to me and wanted to know what happened. I told him. He threatened to get a lawyer. I said, "Colin, a lawyer will cost you a lot more than seven brooms." I am not sure how I get in the middle of things. When I am approached by someone on the street, I just cannot ignore them. If they ask for money, I at least talk to them like a human person. I just cannot walk by like I do not see them. I know that is dangerous, but I cannot shut myself off that way.

Independence Day—August 30

I tried to go to the 5 p.m. show of *Independence Day* at St. Lucia Mall, but the show was sold out. Instead, I bought a ticket for the 7:30 p.m. show and walked around the mall for a while. Then I decided to go to the beach. I was standing on a path overlooking Umhlanga Beach. It was getting dark. No one was around. I was just watching the waves coming in. After a while, I was humming a refrain to a song, *Father, I put my life in your hands.*[44] Inside my head, I could hear the words. Out of the corner of my eye, I saw a man coming toward me. He was a black South African, small build, jaunty walk, wearing a red pull on cap and a dark jacket. In his hand was a pipe. When our eyes made contact, he said very cheerily, "Good evening. That's right, trust in God. Look at it out there. Trust in God." As he walked into the darkness, I felt that his voice and manner were familiar. I had the weirdest feeling that this was someone I knew.[45] It was like something out of that TV program, *Touched by an Angel*. The experience was strictly about spirit not sight.

Eventually, I went back to the mall and the movie. Next to the movie theater was a pizza place. While I waited to go into the evening show, I watched the waiters and waitresses dance out into the mall in a line and sing to someone on their birthday. It was like being at a Pizza Hut in the States. Finally, I went to the movie. In my opinion, it was not as great as the critics made it out to be. The visual effects were good, but I could not understand why all these people were so happy at the end when several large US cities had been destroyed and

---

[44] John Michael Talbot, Album: *Quiet Reflections* (1988)

[45] Perhaps my experience was somehow related to déjà vu. That name is French and means "already seen." Some scientists are intrigued by this phenomenon. Their research has included brain scans. So far, results have produced only theories. In my case, the voice and mannerisms of the stranger reminded me of a friend, Fr. Clem Burghoff. He died on 6 December 1994. Whether he was incognito that day on Umhlanga Beach or never really left paradise, I hope he is praying for me as my earthly journey continues!

nuclear bombs had been released into the atmosphere. It required a suspension of belief!

Hluhluwe—August 31 to September 1

On the spur of the moment, I decided to drive to Hluhluwe on Saturday. I called and reserved a rondavel. The rondavels have no bathroom, but they are very cheap, about $21 US at the current exchange rate. The reservationist knows me by now and she assured me that I would like it—bathroom or no bathroom. I reached Hluhluwe at about 1 p.m. On the way in, I saw two rhinos sitting in a mud puddle. I had never seen them on that side of the park. That turned out to be a good omen because I had a great day of game viewing. When I went to the rondavel, zebras were walking around. I loved it. I told the desk clerk, "If I have to choose between a bathroom and a zebra, I'll take the zebra." That night I had to use my torch to go to the community bathroom. The showers and bathrooms were very clean. When I headed back to the rondavel, I switched off the flashlight and just marveled at the stars. So brilliant in the black sky!

In the morning I decided to leave by a different route than I had planned. That turned out to be a real stroke of luck. I came across a herd of elephants. It is rare to even see one elephant in Hluhluwe, and even rarer to see them close-up. At one point, I came around a bend and saw two elephants mating. I could not believe it! On the other side of the road were two male elephants fighting. An elephant crossed in front of my car. I happened to look in my rear-view mirror and saw another elephant come out of the bush. It was exciting but dangerous to be hemmed in that way. The tourist information tells you to avoid getting close to the elephants. When you stumble upon them, as I did, there is not much you can do but sit back and enjoy these magnificent creatures, and hope they will not take exception to you.

On the way back to Durban, I was stopped by another roadblock. I asked the officers if there had been a robbery. They just wanted to see my license. I told them I had a US license. The first officer slowly enunciated each syllable in Missouri. After that, the second officer said, "Can I see it?" Then the first officer asked, "Have you got a firearm?" I told him, "No, do I need one?" Just another day in paradise!

Say Cheese—September 2

After Mass, I asked Barry Woods and two of the nuns to go outside and let me take their pictures. For a while, Barry stood on the top steps to the rectory, while I and the sisters were in the garden. Finally, I said, "Please, Lord, come down among us." That started him laughing and I snapped two good pictures. I am sure all of them like to have pictures to send to family or friends once in a while.

Weavers Nest—September 3

On my walk to work, I went by the library. I like to go this way because there is a tree that has a dozen or more weavers nests. The nests look like big pieces of fruit hanging from the tip of a branch, drawing it down with their weight. For a long time, I watched these beautiful birds, yellow and black. They get into their nest through a hole in the bottom. One of the nests was curious. The original nest had an oval shape, but built onto it was an annex—a cylinder about six inches long. From my vantage point, I had a good view of the top of the tree. Eventually, I walked down the steps to the sidewalk. There I saw a weaver nest that had fallen. Students were walking by, paying no notice. I picked it up. It was so beautiful and tightly woven with green grass and dried brown grass. I finally placed it under the tree to protect it. In the evening, when I walked home, I went by the tree and picked up the nest to bring it back to the apartment. Then I put it on my balcony, so I could pick it up and look at it sometimes.

A Hen and Her Chicks—September 4

I walked back to the flat from the biology department. On one side of the path, the ground drops away and there is a slope of brush, ending in a campus roadway. On the other side is a fenced-in building that is an on-campus reservoir. A mother hen was leading thirteen baby chicks. A couple of the chicks darted in and out of the chain-link fence. As soon as their mother took off in another direction, they were quick to jump back through the fence and hurry after her. Jesus had a keen eye for that image too. "Jerusalem . . . how often I have longed to gather your children together, as a hen gathers her chicks under her wings, and you were not willing."[46] I hope God still has an eye on his chicks here on earth—all of them.

Film Editing—September 5

In the morning, I gave Barry Woods the pictures of him and the two nuns. Later I brought in the second batch of pictures for the kids at Mkuhla House. I gave the boy who took the picture with my camera the snapshot he created. He did a great job. I focused the camera, but he framed the picture and was right on. I hope he understood enough English to know I was telling him that he did a wonderful job.

Today, I had my Zulu book with me (a child's book). I asked two boys to help me pronounce some of the words, but they wanted to play with a toy. "Okay, no Zulu lesson today," I laughed. "Have fun." Then I went across the room, took the book, and started going through it. Both of the boys came over. One sat on the edge of the upholstered chair and put his arm around me. Without prompting, he pointed

---

[46] Luke 13:34 NIV

to a word and pronounced it. Then the other boy pointed to another word and said it for me. It was so sweet, as though they did not want to hurt my feelings—even though they had not.

After a while, Rose brought over a radio watch that someone had donated. It was in a box and she did not want the two older boys to see it because then they would want it. Their eyes pleaded with me and I opened the box. Each one, in turn, tried on the watch. As it turned out, it was not a new watch; it was broken. I am not sure why people donate broken toys, as though broken is good enough as long as the toy is free. I told Rose that children's digital watches are cheap now, and perhaps we could go buy some for the older kids. Of course, I wish I had brought some from the US.

One of the older boys began playing catch with one of the volunteers. It was difficult for him to even move because his legs were bent at the knees at a 45-degree angle. I asked Rose to walk up the block with me to look at the bikes. I want to buy one for the older children when they come to Mkuhla House. While we were walking, I asked her about the boy I had seen. She said he was a hemophiliac. Immediately, I thought of a boy I went to high school with, Mike Peters. He was a hemophiliac and walked the same way. I had forgotten but the image of him came back to me right away. Rose said it was unlikely the boy would live to his teens. No one expected Mike to finish high school either, but he did. In Africa, though, this boy would not have the same treatment available; it would be too expensive.

In the afternoon, I sat down with Alan Amory's new hardware and software and tried to edit the film Mohammed shot in Silver Glen. I did not have a clue what I was doing, but I managed to extract a clip from the videotape, digitize it, compress it, and store it on the PC as an AVI file (audio/video interleaved). It was a clip of two songbirds feeding on nectar in some blossoms. Now I have to teach myself how to take audio from one portion of the film and join it to video from another portion. It is amazing what you can do on these PCs. I would love to watch something like Jurassic Park in production.

Database Meeting—September 6

In the morning, I recorded at Tape Aids for the Blind from 8 a.m. until 10:45 a.m., an unusually long session. We were doubling up the recording session to Wednesday and Friday to make sure I get this book finished before I return to the US. Mabel said my voice is so distinctive that there is no way they could get someone to "patch" the rest if I did not finish the recording. So, the pressure is on, I guess.

In the afternoon, Michael Berjak drove up from Pietermaritzburg. I met with Mike, Pat, and Norman and discussed how I am going to complete this prototype database before I leave. To do that, I need their input. It is their system, not mine. They discussed again how badly they want me to stay on, but funding is the problem. The Rand falls lower all the time.

Taking Care of Business—September 7

I spent a quiet Saturday. First, I needed to do grocery shopping. When I came back to the campus, I talked for a while with Sipho, Grace, and Magdela, the security guards. Each of them wants to find different jobs. They work twelve-hour days with no benefits, no health insurance, and no pension. Their salary is 900 Rand a month, about $200 US. For their job, they are issued two white shirts and one black uniform, so every night they have to wash out a spare out-fit. Plus, they said that some of the visitors for students on campus have threatened to shoot them. I tried to encourage them, told them not to lose hope, and to get more education if they can. They said that is impossible. By the time they finish their twelve-hour shift, they are tired and some of them have families that need attention. They are going to give me their résumés and I will word-process them on my Macintosh. Maybe this will help. Also, I will keep my ears open in case I hear of a job. Dave and Isabel at the car rental agency might know of something.

This afternoon, I worked on my résumé. There was an ad on the Internet yesterday with the American Association for the Advancement of Science. They are looking for a director for the sub-Saharan Africa program.

At Mass this evening, we had an OMI who grew up in Assumption Parish. He made his First Communion there in 1962. Now he is a missionary in Zimbabwe. His name is Paul and he was the altar boy when Derrick Butt first came to Assumption Parish soon after his ordination in 1971. Derrick is now the pastor at Assumption. I enjoyed Paul's sermon. It was about his experience in Zimbabwe. He was sent to a rural area where he did not know the language and where there was no Christian community. That is pretty tough. The attitude of the church has changed toward missionaries. In many cases, there is more respect for the local culture—or should be, at any rate. I remember reading somewhere about Charles de Foucauld who went out into the desert with the Bedouin. He was not there to convert them, but simply to be a Christian presence among them and to follow his desert call. Gandhi supposedly said to one of his ardent Christian friends that the way to become a better Christian was to help him become a better Hindu. That is not verbatim but it captures the gist of Gandhi's words. I like that idea.

Mooi River—September 8

At 9:30 a.m. this Saturday, I drove up to Mooi River. Debbie Walsh, a part-time computer support person in the biology department, invited me to come up for a "braai" with her family. Every year, her family spends two weeks at the Midlands Saddle and Trout Club on a timeshare basis. Debbie was there; her husband, John; her brother Dave; her sister-in-law, Glenda; her mom, Margaret; her dad; and four kids that were four years old or younger. Debbie has two boys and is expecting a new baby in March. Glenda has a boy and a girl. They did not start what Americans would call a barbeque until 2:30 p.m.

and I had to leave at 3:00 p.m. It's a two-hour drive back to Durban. There were T-bone steaks and bratwurst, but, since I have given up meat, I just had vegetables—baked potato, asparagus, beans, and creamed corn. Also, I brought up two packs of Coca-Cola, something American for the feast.

Before lunch, we walked around the grounds. Matthew, age three, asked his grandmother to tell him what happens when you die. I am sure he heard the family talking about the fact that Dave's mother had died of emphysema on Monday. His grandmother said, "Jesus comes and takes you to heaven and you become a star in the sky." She hardly had the words out of her mouth, when Matthew said, "I'll look for you at night, grandma." Matthew does not know it, but this grandma has emphysema too. She is a heavy smoker. Earlier, Annie, age three or four, saw an airplane in the sky and said, "That plane is gonna pick up grandma and bring her back to us."

We walked to a paddock where some beautiful horses were grazing. Debbie explained that they were retired racehorses; the timeshare club uses them for riding. Matthew kept shooting an imaginary gun at them. "Look, Mom," he said. "I'm gonna shoot that horse over there now." I said, "Oh, Matthew, you don't want to shoot the horses." Bang. Bang. Bang. You wonder what is going on in those little brains.

Marches and Mayhem—September 9

The students were on the march again today. We received notice at about 10:30 a.m. that the campus was on red alert. All doors were locked. No one could get in or out of the biology building. From my office window, I saw students running out of the physics building and through the courtyard that is between the biology and physics buildings. Following the running students were some marching and chanting students. They had sticks in their hands. Later we heard what had happened. The marchers were protesting the election of a white student to the student government. They smashed cars and tore up the cafeteria and other buildings. Alan Amory's windshield was broken. Someone else had rocks thrown at him. Classes were canceled for today and tomorrow. I was supposed to go to a party tonight from 6:30 p.m. to 8:30 p.m. in North Durban. It was a party for the new US Consul. For various reasons, I decided to pass. It is dark here at 6 p.m. There is no parking at the Consul's home, only parking in the street. Since I was on my own, it did not seem a good idea to be walking alone at night. Plus, the party was one of those see-and-be-seen affairs.

Today, I had two meetings. One was with Pat and Norman, another with Wayne Twine and Dehn. I am still trying to pin them down on the specifications for this ethnobotanical database. The whole afternoon was spent working with software for editing film. It is kind of fun.

More Meetings—September 10

All lectures were canceled today because of the violence yesterday. Some students were arrested. When I walked into work this morning, I heard the students chanting again by the Student Union Building, something like, "Drum it up, drum it up." Later we heard that the students went in buses to the police station to protest the arrests. Meanwhile, it was cleanup time on the campus.

I had a meeting at 11 a.m. with Pat, Wayne, Dehn, and John Cooke, the head of the biology department. It was about the database I am prototyping. Pat told me later that John wants his top priority to be finding money for me to return next year. We will see. The rest of the day I spent working with Media Studio 2, learning how to edit film and create video computer files. It was fun and I was amazed at what I could do. I just go at it intuitively: no manuals, no tutorials, and no classes. None of those are available to me. One good thing about this project is that I am forced to do a variety of things, for example, design a database, scan photos, edit images, supervise filming, edit films, and interview local experts for their knowledge. I have become a whole project team. Come December, I know I am going to be tired.

As usual, I went to 5:30 p.m. Mass at Assumption. Afterward, Ray, one of the men in the parish, came running out to my car. "Where have you been?" he said. "I've been so worried about you." Since I was going to 7 a.m. Mass at the OMI Provincial House, I had not been to the morning Mass at the parish for a while. Nice to know someone misses you!

Friday— September 13

This morning I went to Tape Aids for the Blind. The end is finally in sight for *The Client*. Tim, the editor, asked me to patch two places in the tape because I pronounced the word "route" like rout rather than root. He said South Africans would not know what I meant. Then there was a discussion about how to pronounce Roosevelt. I pronounced it Row-za-velt, rather than Roo-za-velt. Tim looked up the word in an American pronunciation guideline and said the first pronunciation was the one that Franklin Roosevelt used. The organization is very intent that everything is correct. Tim said they could not duplicate an American accent, but mine was "so manifestly American" that it suited the book perfectly.

This sad story was on the news. A mother dolphin and her calf beached themselves in East London (South Africa). A man from the town hacked the mother to death and left the calf. Conservationists put the calf in a tank and encouraged it to feed and swim. It refused. They finally killed it with an injection.

Fighting a Cold—September 14 and 15th

This weekend I spent in bed with a cold. I thought I would get rid of it faster if I let my body rest. Since I have been in Africa, I have come down with quite a few colds. Maybe it is a matter of my body adjusting to new germs. This evening I went to the Youth Mass at Assumption. Someone plays the guitar and there are a lot of the Jesuit songs, such as *Here I Am, Lord* and *Of My Hands, I Give to You, O Lord*.

When I returned from Mass, I turned on the TV and caught the tail end of a nature program. It was interesting. The film was about a baboon troop near a community in Kenya. Two of the baboons picked up pieces of a broken mirror. They were fascinated by their image and would not let go of their newfound treasure. Another baboon picked up a piece of a windowpane. Then he licked it with his tongue to clean off the dirt and moved it at different angles until he could see his re-flection. The point of the narration was asking whether these baboons recognize the reflection as their own. Do they have self-knowledge? I have no idea, but it was fascinating to watch them.

Reading the Sunday paper, I can see that Mandela is taking some flak. Until now, it has been all adulation since he stepped out of prison. A couple of weeks ago, he announced plans to live with Graca Machel, the widow of the first president of Mozambique.[47] Samora Machel died in a plane crash in 1986. Mandela has been married twice and divorced twice. There were opinions in the paper about whether he should marry. Even Desmond Tutu had something to say. He thinks they should marry. Mandela is 78 years old. I am sure he can make up his mind. He says in his autobiography that religion never played a big part in his life; politics did. So, I do not think he is worried about the opinion of the clergy. Besides, Tutu is an Anglican and Mandela is a Methodist. Mandela is beginning to take heat for his politics these days too. Some people feel nothing is being done about the violence and the crime, that his criticism of F. W. de Klerk is turning vicious, and that his judgment is blinded by ANC loyalty.

---

[47] Mandela married Graca Machel on his 80th birthday, 18 July 1998. On 5 December 2013, Mandela died at the age of 95. Machel has received awards over the years as an advocate for the rights of women and children, including refugee children. She has worked for the United Nations and its agency, UNESCO (United Nations Educational, Scientific and Cultural Organization).

Thabo Mbeki is already being pushed into the limelight as the new successor to Mandela.

Cold Continues—September 16

Today I am home with a cold again. I slept a lot and also wrote a few letters.

Doctor Visit—September 18

This morning I called the biology office and got the name of a doctor, Michael Goodall. He is in Musgrave Park, the same place as my dentist. I called at 9:15 a.m. and made an appointment for 10:15 a.m. The letters behind his name on the door were MB and Ch.B.[48] I do not know what this means. Does this mean he is a Bachelor of Medicine as opposed to a Doctor of Medicine? Anyway, I am assured that all general practitioners have these letters behind their names. Dr. Goodall was super nice. At first, all we talked about was my upcoming trip to Namibia. He pulled out his prescription pad and started writing. "You must go," he said. "You must go there." While continuing to write, he was wistfully recalling trips to Namibia and saying he must go back. Finally, he said he would put some information together for me and fax it. He was much more laid back than most American doctors I have run into. Plus, he had time just to talk. After that, he did his exam: looked in my ears; looked in my throat; listened to my lungs with his stethoscope. "Doesn't sound too horrible," he said. Then he listened to my heart. From his cabinet, he took out a packet of Penicillin and Demazin to dry up my nose. The total cost was 160 Rand or about $34 US by the current exchange rate. You cannot beat it! When I left Dr. Goodall's office, I ran a few errands and then spent the rest of the day in bed, resting.

---

[48] Bachelor of Medicine (Medicinae Baccalaureus) and Bachelor of Surgery (Chirurgiae Baccalaureus)

September 19

I am still taking antibiotics, but I went to work from 4:30 p.m. to 6:00 p.m. to help Pat Berjak put together a proposal for a funding group.

September 20

My cold hangs on. I phoned the doctor on call and told him I was taking Augmentin and Demazin. He said there was nothing more to do but let it run its course. That may be the primary function of doctors—reassurance.

September 21

I did some shopping and packing for my upcoming trip.

September 22

Around 5 p.m., I discovered that I could not find my passport. I phoned Pat Berjak, and then tried to find the telephone number for the US Consul. No luck. Finally, I drove out to Paul Denig's house. We hopped in Paul's car and drove to Scott Hamilton's house. Scott is a lawyer with the consulate. At that moment, he was entertaining a woman, so we talked in his front driveway. Scott said he could issue me a temporary passport at 8 a.m. That was the best he could do. Of course, I would miss my Monday morning flight to Windhoek. After I left Paul at his house, I was determined to keep searching for the missing passport. On the way home, I prayed to St. Anthony, the patron saint of lost articles. Within ten minutes of hitting the front door, I found the passport.

September 23—Trip to Namibia

I left for the airport at 6:15 a.m. and arrived so early that I could have made the 7 a.m. flight. From Durban to Johannesburg, I talked to a young woman sitting next to me. She was a travel agent on the way to London.

At Windhoek Airport, I rented a car with a stick shift. Automatics were twice as much. I made it to Pension Kleines Heim with no problem. Immediately, I was greeted by an overweight Rottweiler with a useless front leg. Perhaps she was hit by a car at one time. Loka was her name.

September 24—Tuesday

I left for Etosha[49] at about 7:20 a.m. During the drive, I listened to music on the radio: Surfin' U.S.A; Drop Dead Beautiful; something about a fellow who wants to make love in his car or to his car. It was Country Western.

When I arrived in Etosha, it was about 11:30 a.m. My accommodation was at Okaukuejo Camp. There were two rooms: a kitchen/living room and a bedroom with three beds. Above one of the beds was a nice picture of a lion.

I spent from 6:30-11:00 a.m. at the waterhole. There were lots of elephants, rhinos, zebras, giraffes, and jackals. The elephants had the first choice at the waterhole. They chased away other animals

---

[49] Etosha National Park in Namibia is among the largest national parks in Africa. Etosha pan comprises about one-quarter of the entire park. The name pan refers to natural hollows or basins in the ground in which water can collect. After the water has evaporated, a deposit of salt can remain. Etosha is the largest salt pan in Africa. In the language of the Ovambo, primarily native to Namibia, Etosha means "great white place." The salt and sun turn the land dazzling white; sunglasses are definitely not a fashion statement in Etosha. The park is known for its waterholes where animals gather, along with attracted tourists. In the park, there are natural water holes and those which were created through digging or boreholes.

who dared to approach. The elephants looked two-toned. The part of their body that was splashed with water was dark and the rest was light. A thirsty rhino finally approached the waterhole. To get out of an elephant's way, the rhino went into the water. Then the elephant would not let the rhino get out. They were like partners in a dance—never touching but the movement of one determined the movement of the other.

When the elephants finish drinking, they step into the water and bathe. In the process, they muddy the waters! The other animals just stay back in the bush and watch—and wait.

September 25

This morning around 9 a.m., I left for Numatoni Camp. Across one flat plain, I saw four antelopes walking, with sun rays coming down behind them. Beautiful!

The waterhole at Numatoni is overgrown with reeds and smells like sewer water. Maybe it was the sewer of the 19th-century German fort that still stands here.

My room, C1, is very large and very nice. First, I went to the picture window to draw my drapes. Surprise! Some old guy just happened, at that moment, to strip off his swimming suit. He was standing by the pool and trying to put on his long pants, but he could not get his leg in. I shut the drapes so that he could have a modicum of privacy in the great outdoors.

September 26

At about 8:30 a.m., I left for Mokuti Lodge. This is a luxury camp outside Etosha. I had to make a reservation there for one night; nothing was available inside the park.

Driving around Etosha, I saw lots of wildlife—gemsbok, zebra, giraffe, impala, wildebeest, and kudu. At one waterhole, there was a male and female elephant with a baby. A holy elephant family! Also, I saw some elephants on the edge of the bush.

White dust is everywhere. Etosha is a salt pan. At one time, it was a lake. The white dust looks like snow and frost. I even found myself singing "dashing through the snow!"

Before dinner, I talked to one of the black workers. His two children were with him. There was a four-year-old girl named Angel and a four-month-old boy who was drinking from a juice container already. We laughed at how tough that little guy was.

September 27

I watched a springbok drinking at a waterhole. Its delicate body reflected in the water almost looked like a cross-section of a marine shell—the kind people buy in Florida for pendants.

From 1:30 p.m. to 2:30 p.m., I sat at another waterhole. My car was the only one there. About three dozen elephants were in the waterhole, muddying the waters. Big elephant feet were splashing mud on a baby elephant lying in the water. So powerful, but so gentle! When the elephants stepped out of the waterhole, they used the white dust as a dusting powder. All the elephants created such a cloud of dust that they were almost invisible—like an octopus squirting ink. Giraffes and zebras waited for their turn to take a drink. I could hear the sound of the zebra hooves. The elephants split into two herds. As they lay down on the ground, it looked like there had been a great battle!

At sunset by another waterhole, I saw two elephants playing in the water. One of the elephants submerged its head. I counted the seconds: . . . 12, 13, 14.

Then the tip of the elephant's trunk came out of the water like a snorkel. Above the trees I could see the heads of giraffes, waiting for a chance to drink. One elephant came toward my car. I moved as quickly as I could.

September 28

Today I drove to Kakheuwel, a man-made water hole. There were lots of animals, but the film in my camera was not wound properly. Next, I drove to Halali and, in the evening, to Tsumcor. Both are also water holes. At Tsumcor, I watched kudu drinking, the water streaming from their mouths.

September 29

I left Namutoni around 6:45 a.m. At Kakheuwel, I spotted more wildlife. Then I arrived at Okakauejo around 12:30 and had some lunch and rest. At 3:45 p.m., I went out again. On the way to Olifants, I saw a lioness under a tree. It was just a glimpse. At Olifants, I saw a lion and a lioness lying side by side and the tip of the head of another lion about twenty feet away.

I stayed at the waterhole inside the camp until about 9:30 p.m. Thirteen elephants came by. A baby elephant went into the water to drink and then had trouble getting out. He kept slipping and sliding back into the water. In the moonlight, the skin of the elephants looked like crushed satin. One of the large elephants submerged in the water and put its trunk up like a snorkel. Off to one side of the waterhole were four rhinos—two males, a female, and a baby. The baby got under the momma. If she sat down, she would have been sitting on the baby's horn. Ouch! She appeared to be protecting the baby from the males. There were real face-offs. When the rhinos went to drink, there were perfect reflections of them in the water. A full reflection of a large elephant would have been too big for the waterhole!

September 30

I drove onto the pan itself. The road extends for some distance onto the dry, cracked lake bed and then ends in a circle. You can look back at the bush. The heat is intense. Nothing lives or walks out there on the pan. It is amazing how healthy the animals at Etosha look despite the harsh conditions. I believe the sufferings of the animals, the cruelties and pain they endure, are part of the redemptive act as much as our suffering. I probably could never get a certificate as a Catholic theologian! Maybe a Buddhist monk though. No, women cannot be Buddhist monks. A certified monkey then!

In the afternoon, I headed to Windhoek, the largest city in Namibia, with a stopover in Omaruru. Michael Goodall recommended Hotel Straebe. Omarur is near Mount Erongo. Supposedly, this is the only place on earth where a certain species of dung beetle is found. When I opened the trunk of my car, there was elephant dung that I had picked up somewhere along the way for a souvenir. I joked that I was going to give my brother one lump for Christmas! What I did not realize was that the dung housed dozens of dung beetles. They were not visible when I picked up the dung. Now they were all over the trunk of the car and all over my suitcases. I became concerned about the survival of the dung beetles because there were no elephants or dung in sight! I gathered them up and took them to a nearby field, with the hope that they would survive—rare or not. Trying to correct mistakes can be futile when we humans stumble into the wild or introduce a species into a new environment.

That evening, with mistakes put behind me, I had a great dinner at the hotel. The meal was beautifully presented as well as delicious.

October 1

Today I drove back to Windhoek via the scenic route recommended by the owner of the hotel. I was opening and shutting livestock gates to make my way. At one point, I simply stopped at a cattle station and honked my horn. I did not go through the front gate because there were some guard dogs. Finally, a lady came out. I told her, "I'm beginning to wonder if I'm lost!" She assured me that I was on the right road if you could call it that. Of course, she recognized my accent and wanted to know where I was from. I told her if I ran out of gas on this long-deserted road, I was going to hike back to her place. She said I would be welcome.

Eventually, I picked up the main highway to Windhoek. All along the road was a raised pipe that looked like a gas or oil line. With all the dunes around me and the oil line, I might as well have been in Saudi Arabia.

In Windhoek, I stayed at a place that had been a nursing home. There were still nursing home guests in a building behind the main building. The door to my room was huge. I was told that they used to move hospital beds in and out of the room. There was a card in my room advising me to be quiet between 1 and 3 p.m. because that was naptime!

Windhoek

I spent a couple of days in Windhoek and had a great meal at a restaurant right on the ocean. At one time it was a tug boat, called *The Tug*. The restaurant was on two levels and the seating capacity was very limited. I had reserved a seat right at the window and took a long time over dinner just so I could enjoy the ocean waves rushing toward the beach. The waiter told me not to hurry because the table was reserved for me for the evening. Afterward, I went out on the nearby walkway that extended quite a distance into the water. Originally, it was intended to go out about a quarter of a mile. Because it was very cold, I did not linger too long.

On two mornings, I went to Mass at the local Catholic Church. It was all in German. The priest and the nuns (all old) were from Germany as well.

October 8 to November 24

Since returning from Etosha, I have been occupied with work and packing. Of course, there were trips to the beach, the occasional movie, and Zulu classes.

December 14

I am spending my last few days in South Africa in one of God's wild spaces. No surprise to you, I am sure! It is 9 p.m. and outside there is rain, thunder, and lightning. I am sitting propped up in my bed with my laptop on my lap. In this electrical storm, it would not be wise to plug in my Macintosh to a wall outlet. It might get zapped. I might get zapped with it! So, I'm running on battery power. I started a hand-written letter, but the lights keep going on and off. There is something good to be said about modern technology. I might have to use this laptop as a night light too! That is about as feeble a use for computer chips as I can think of.

I just could not resist reporting back one last time before I left the African continent with more unconfirmed God-sightings! Truly, when I see these wonderful animals and these beautiful green hills, sometimes I sing for God right in the car and sometimes I just tell him "I love you" and "Thank you, God." I even talk to the animals (an American Dr. Doolittle). I tell them how beautiful they are and how they give God glory. They move off into the bush as if to say, "Yes, we know."

It is not all pretty. Early in the morning, I saw this gorgeous zebra by the side of the road. I stopped to take its picture. A few yards further down the road was a young zebra, obviously waiting for it. Then I saw that the adult zebra had a broken front ankle. It was dangling from its leg. Soon it might be lion meat and probably its youngster too. Or it would die of thirst because it could not make it to a water-hole. Eventually spotting a park ranger, I told him about the zebras and where they were located in the hope that at least the young zebra could be saved. Deep down, I thought the ranger would likely shoot the wounded zebra because of his training or his compassion.

In the late afternoon, I saw three rhinos sleeping in a water-hole. As they breathed in and out, they made bubbles in the water. Remember as a kid when you use to take a straw and blow bubbles in your milk or Kool-Aid? Sometimes I still do. Friends cannot take me anywhere! As I watched those snoozing rhinos, it was as though I could feel God's sweetness blowing through me and his laughter bubbling up. God is so real to me. As I come to understand that He is not real to so many people, I thank Him for this smell and taste of Him in my soul. Does that sound crazy? Do not answer that!

This morning I gave a ride to three Zulu workers who were try-ing to get from Memorial Gate to Hilltop Camp—a 17 km stretch of road. They just came up to my car, stopped at the crossbar, and asked for a lift. Their names were Elijah, Princess, and Habit. Among Zulus, you hear a wonderful variety of names, like Knowledge and Happiness. Habit, though, kind of threw me. I am curious if he was named for a good habit or a bad habit, or if he was just conceived out of habit. The mind puzzles over what this could mean.

Anyway, I drove slowly and stopped so my passengers could enjoy the animals too. I told them I was their American tour guide. We laughed at a troop of baboons, including a tiny baby, and we uttered Oohs and Aahs at the the giraffes. In between, I asked about them and the "new South Africa." It was an unexpected grace to share some time with them—along with three donuts I had just bought at the bakery, not knowing I was going to have three guests. God must have known. God also knew that no way did I need to eat those donuts. So, I was relieved of them!

While I lived in South Africa, I learned a new Nguni word: Masakhane. "Let us build one another." It is in this spirit that I tell these stories—to give others the courage to build people up and love deeply for God.

COSTAL ELEPHANTS – SOUTH AFRICA

ZEBRAS – ETOSHA PAN, NAMIBIA

AUTHOR IN SOUTH AFRICA – A LIFETIME AGO

12

BROTHER GIOVANNI

Some might prepare for an ordinary day, but for Brother Giovanni, there is no such thing. How could there be? There were new people to meet and new adventures ahead. Even the familiar people were never the same. They wake up on different days—some sunny, some rainy, some grumpy, some happy. Each day was different in some way.

Had he been a soaring eagle with an eagle's keen sight, Brother Giovanni could have spotted that instantly. Some rivers had wiggled just slightly to the left or to the right. Some creatures had moved from one home to another. Some trees had fallen and some were just beginning to grow. Yes, it was a day different than any day before. No matter where you lived in the world, something had changed this day. How marvelous indeed or perhaps disconcerting and even frightening! Still, let the adventure begin.

I have been Brother Giovanni's partner on his mission and adventures for ten years and, by necessity, a teller of his tales since he speaks only the heartfelt but wordless language of presence. Brother Giovanni, you see, is a *Canis lupus familiaris*. What is that? Well, that is the Latin name that science has given to all dogs. Roughly it means a dog-wolf that is part of the human family.

Fr. Mark Dolan, Brother Giovanni's master, gave him his special name. It can be a mouthful, though, especially when immediate action is required. So, Gio works best for most occasions. Gio, get off the bed. Gio, drop the bunny. Gio, want a piece of bacon?

Of course, there are many different kinds of dogs. As dog nations go, Gio's is rather small but ancient. He is a Hungarian vizsla. Way back—almost 700 years ago—the King of Hungary and his barons used vizslas for hunting. King Louis I of Hungary and Croatia commissioned a chronicle of his land by the Carmelite Friars. The Chronicon Pictum (Illuminated Chronicle) dates before 1360 and is now in the National Széchényi Library in Budapest, Hungary. In a section on falconry, there is an illustration of a vizsla with a royal hunting party. Quite a pedigree!

Gio does not use his instinctive hunting skills to put a wild pheasant or duck on his master's table, but he does chase any squirrel or bunny that crosses his path and pursues their scent when his powerful nose catches the slightest whiff. Once, after Mass on Thanksgiving Day, he staged The Great Squirrel Chase! Gio had come into the church and locked onto a scent. It was not the scent of roses or incense, but the scent of a squirrel. Not only did his human companions not smell the squirrel, but they did not see it either until the chase was on. Gio dashed all over the church in pursuit of the squirrel—around the pillars, under the pews, across the sanctuary, even into the pulpit, where he appeared to be giving a sermon, possibly about squirrels or perhaps directed to one particular squirrel.

Fr. Dolan, Ken (a Knight of Columbus, sans sword), and I managed to pursue the squirrel into the vestibule and close the inside doors to the church. Unfortunately, Gio slipped through one of the doors before it closed. Now he and the squirrel had a smaller area to race around.

For one brief moment, Gio had the squirrel in his mouth. I shouted plaintively ("Gio, no!") and Gio dropped his prey, then decided that was a bad decision and continued the pursuit. Being a universal animal lover, I did not want the squirrel to be hurt. At the first opportunity and with Fr. Dolan's help, we corralled Gio behind an open closet door and a garbage bin. Then I dragged him by his dog collar back into the church through a side door. Gio, of course, was not pleased because, true to his vizsla breed, he was the one who had done all the tracking and hunting up to that point. That left Fr. Dolan, Ken, and me to catch the squirrel.

At one point we thought we had the squirrel captured in a closet; its door still stood open after Gio's banishment. I borrowed a winter glove from Ken, thinking I could pick up the squirrel by its tail while Fr. Dolan had him between a broom and a box. The squirrel was too smart for us and raced out of our trap. Finally, as Ken and I coaxed the squirrel toward the open front door of the church, Fr. Dolan threw an upside-down box over him. Unfortunately, as Fr. Dolan was pushing the box through the open doors and onto the church porch, part of the squirrel's tail came off—just about two inches. However, he did manage to get the squirrel outside and out of danger from Gio, although, from the squirrel's perspective, also out of its warm church residence and with no post-surgery support.

Fr. Dolan gave me the fragment of the squirrel's tail. I felt like a matador claiming the bull's tail as a grizzly trophy. Of course, Fr. Dolan felt bad about the squirrel's missing appendage. I suggested to him that maybe squirrels can release part of their tail when they are trapped by a predator as some lizards can. Umm, probably not! We left the church that day hopeful that the squirrel would be OK even if he would not be able to wave his formerly bushy tale for the spring mating rituals.

Not all of Gio's adventures are so physically robust. Many are adventures of the heart and spirit. Gio is also a therapy dog. Before the COVID-19 pandemic, he went Monday through Thursday to nursing homes, including Mother of Good Counsel, Missouri Veterans Home, Nazareth Living Center, Fusz Pavilion at Jesuit Hall, and Little Sisters of the Poor. All of Gio's visits came to a halt as nursing homes across the city went into quarantine because of COVID. Since Sumer 2021, however, Gio has been able to return to Mother of Good Counsel Home, even though, initially, he could no longer visit patient rooms. Instead, we attended morning Mass three days a week and continue to do so. As residents enter and leave the chapel, Gio approaches each walker or wheelchair to greet them, along with staff members and volunteers. Some of the residents not only pet Gio but have daily words of praise and love. Also, they are eager to let me know, "Gio loves me."

Over the years of Gio's service, there are many stories I have told friends about Gio's ability to reach people that other people cannot reach. Once, after Mass at Mother of Good Counsel when most of the people had passed by and received Gio's full attention, one of the attendants suddenly stopped pushing a wheelchair and went to check on someone else. The wheelchair was about six feet from Gio and me. In the wheelchair was Helen, a petite woman who did not appear to be alert. Gio went up to her and immediately began nuzzling her hand. All of a sudden, Helen reached out to Gio. "Oh, you holy dog," she said. "You are the Church too; you are the Church." Then she lowered her upper body down to her knees and placed her head on Gio's shoulder.

To me, Helen was speaking the truth. At that moment and in that chapel, Gio was the Church, giving comfort to the sick, the lonely, and often, the forgotten. I suspect there is at least one person who would back me up. Richard Rohr, a Franciscan priest, dedicated his book, *The Universal Christ*, to his black Labrador, Venus. "Without any apology, lightweight theology, or fear of heresy," he wrote, "I can appropriately say that Venus was also Christ for me."

Sometimes on our visits to nursing homes, I would take pictures of Gio with his friends. Since a picture can be better than a thousand words, I have included three photos that show a progressive story of the spirit. The man in the photo is Fr. Carl Dehne. Gio and I would visit the Pavilion at Jesuit Hall, where Jesuits needing assistance stayed. Carl always called Gio a "noble dog." Often Carl would just sit and contemplate him. Gio brought Carl his unique comfort up to the time of Carl's death in 2017.

Also, I have included a photo taken by Fr. Dolan several years ago when he and Gio were in church alone. It has always prompted a smile. Gio was raised with love and has never experienced human cruelty. He has spent his life far more among people than dogs. Living in a church rectory, he is accustomed to acceptance and gentleness, even when disciplined. With the help of Fr. Dolan's photo, I suggest the healthy wisdom Gio might pass on to us if he could speak.

Even today, as a senior dog, Gio continues to bring joy and comfort. Throughout my life, I have traveled to many countries and voyaged on oceans. Now my journey is a different one, but no less adventurous. Most importantly, with Gio at my side, I also continue to live in God's laughter.

CARL AND GIO

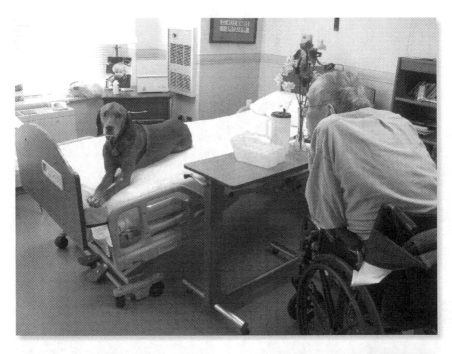

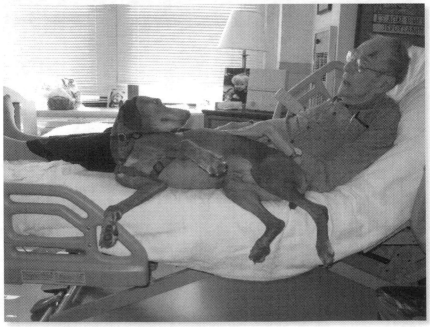

The Gospel According to Brother Giovanni

The way you speak to your dog with praise, encouragement, understanding, forgiveness, gratitude, and even love is the way you should all speak to one another.

POSTSCRIPT

On 11 July 2022, many people around the world saw the first image from the James Webb Space Telescope. It was like an artist's canvas, with dabs and stabs of color on a black background. Only this canvas was a digital snapshot of light traveling from stars and galaxies a million miles from earth. Live transmission showed the international team members, who brought this 30-year-old dream to reality, bursting into cheers and laughter. As I watched, I was filled with awe and laughter too.

If we can see light from stars and galaxies that may no longer exist in this swirling universe, what else can be possible? We wonder. Wonder leads to laughter even among the scientists that delve into the universe with their complicated instruments and explain the unthinkable to us. In doing so, they sometimes brush their thoughts with mystics and theologians. "Christ has a cosmic body," Teilhard de Chardin wrote, "that extends throughout the universe."[50] That thought needs a theologian or mystic to unfold it. I am neither. Perhaps from the earth, our spiritual energy travels out into the universe, as well. Maybe our laughter will even mix with the laughter of God!

---

[50] See *Cosmic Life*, 1916, XII, 58. Teilhard de Chardin (1881-1955) was a French Jesuit priest whose interests included science, paleontology, theology, and philosophy. As an undergraduate at St. Louis University, I was introduced to Teilhard's work by a prolific Jesuit scholar and author, Walter Ong. Teilhard used the term *noosphere* to denote "the thinking layer of the earth." With my interest in computers and technology, I wrote an article called the *Electronic Noosphere* (The Teilhard Journal, England, 1980). Unlike the enduring work of Teilhard and Ong, my article has likely disappeared from both the earth and the noosphere!

Printed in the United States
by Baker & Taylor Publisher Services